Liz Dobbs

special photography by
Craig Knowles

tools for
gardeners

jacqui
small

To my parents, Jack and Barbara

First published in 2002 by Jacqui Small,
an imprint of Aurum Press Ltd,
25 Bedford Avenue, London WC1B 3AT

Publisher Jacqui Small
Editorial Director Stuart Cooper
Art Director Robin Rout
Photoshoot Production Assistant
Audrey Crummay
Production Geoff Barlow

British Library Cataloguing-in-
Publication Data
A catalogue record for this book is
available from the British Library

ISBN 1-903221-07-2

Printed and bound in China

2004 2003 2002
10 9 8 7 6 5 4 3 2 1

storing tools

Long-handled hand tools are best hung on hooks in a garage, shed or cupboard indoors, so they are off the ground – hang them head up or head down, whichever you prefer. If you do not have a suitable wall for hooks, a section of trellis and a few meat hooks make a good substitute. Alternatively, if you do not have an outbuilding where you can store tools, and there is no space indoors, invest in an outdoor wooden or metal tool cupboard or a wooden storage box that doubles as a bench. Smaller hand tools, especially those you use often such as secateurs, a trowel, a knife and a handweeder can be stored in a bag, bucket or trug. Add some raffia, garden twine, a few labels and a pencil – you will then have a portable tool-kit for a session of pruning, tying in, weeding and labelling. Small knives and scissors that are used infrequently are best kept indoors with kitchen tools. Indoors is also the best place to keep fabric gloves or fabric kneelers; they often go mouldy when stored in a garden shed or garage. Small plant ties, labels and rolls of wire can be kept in tins or drawers. Drawers or plastic storage boxes with lids are also good for storing folded netting, fleece or bubble insulation.

At the end of the watering season, dismantle watering systems and store them carefully, particularly small emitters. Water timers are best stored indoors; remove the batteries before storing and insert new ones at the start of the next season. Coil up loose hoses and hang them out of the way.

Containers will last longer if stored under cover, as this will reduce the effects of weathering. When moving containers, take care not to chip or crack them. Containers made of porous materials such as terracotta are less likely to crack if they are stored empty, so stack pots on their sides, or turn single pots or window boxes on their sides to prevent them from filling with water.

Safety matters
For safety's sake, close the blades of any sharp cutting tools before storing them. Use the safety catch if there is one, or put the blade in a scabbard, holster or other protector. Power equipment should be stored in a dry place under cover where people will not bump into or trip over it. Electric cable often gets damaged if it is left trailing, so store it carefully or the tool could be dangerous next time you use it. Keep safety gear such as ear defenders, goggles and an RCD (residual current device) near the tool, so you remember to use them, but keep them somewhere they will not get knocked or scratched.

Bamboo canes should be stored safely. Either put them in a section of drainpipe laid on a shelf or tie them in bundles, prop them up in a bucket and cover the tops with an old plant pot. Other plant supports are best dismantled and hung up.

Hanging long-handled hand tools on hooks means you can see what you need at a glance, and raising the heads off the ground reduces the likelihood of rusting.

Space-saving tools
If storage space is limited, consider an interchangeable tool system. The beauty of these is that you buy one handle at a length that suits you, and add different heads as required for raking, hoeing, weeding pruning and other tasks. Other advantages are that the heads can be detached from the handles for easier cleaning, and transporting the tools, to an allotment for example, is much easier. If you share tools with other people, the ability to mix and match handles and tool heads means everyone can have tools that suit them.

There are a few limitations to such systems: you must stick with one brand, and initially the systems are quite expensive. The attachments are either snap-in or screw-in, and it is worth trying them out in the shop to see which you prefer, as well as checking the range of tool heads available.

There are currently two main interchangeable tool systems, made by Wolf and Gardena. The Wolf system has eight handle lengths in various materials with snap-lock fixings. There are around 40 tool heads, mostly soil cultivators, weeders, rakes and lawn tools. In addition to metal tool heads, there are now also lighter-weight plastic polymer versions. The Gardena system includes a range of wooden and aluminium handles measuring 130–150cm, a telescopic handle and an extension handle that extends to 78cm. There are about 20 small tool heads and over 40 large ones.

Attachments for interchangeable systems are shown in the relevant chapters.

material choice

This section gives brief descriptions of the principal materials used for making gardening tools, and lists their pros and cons. It is mainly concerned with hand tools, which appear throughout the book. Materials used for other items such as plant labels, watering equipment, containers, weather protectors and plant supports are described in the relevant chapters.

This section also outlines the different processes used in the manufacture of metal tools, as these have a dramatic impact on the strength and durability of the finished product.

CARBON STEEL
An alloy of iron with a small amount of carbon.
Uses Widely used for tool heads, including spades, hoes and half-moon cutters. Carbon steel made with added manganese will bend slightly without breaking, so is often used for digging and border forks. Carbon steel is sometimes painted or coated with zinc to prevent rust, although the coating can wear off.
Pros It is easy to file the edge of a blade to sharpen it. Tools are usually less expensive than stainless-steel versions, although the price gap is narrowing.
Cons Tools need to be regularly wiped with an oily rag to prevent them from rusting. They must be stored in a dry place.

STAINLESS STEEL
Carbon steel with the addition of chromium and nickel, which make the tools rustproof, although they can still become stained on the surface if left outside.
Uses Widely used for tool heads, particularly for digging, cultivating and planting tools.
Pros Cuts through sticky soil more easily. Easy to clean – dirt can be simply wiped off with a damp cloth. Does not rust.
Cons Good-quality stainless-steel tools are expensive; cheap tools are prone to bending. It is harder to sharpen an edge on a stainless-steel tool.

ALUMINIUM
Aluminium described as 'anodized' has been treated chemically to make it hard and weather resistant.
Uses Handle shafts, often tubular rather than solid. Tool heads in which lightness is more important than strength, for example the heads of shovels and scoops.
Pros A lightweight metal, it makes long-handled tools like pole pruners more manageable. It is also useful for small tools where a single piece of metal can form the handle and head.
Cons In winter, the tool will feel cold unless you wear gloves.

WOOD
Hardwoods are used for handles, and may be left untreated or coated with varnish or paint. Ash or hickory are good choices as they are strong yet not brittle; however, often the type of wood is not stated on the label. Unvarnished handles can be rubbed with linseed oil to protect the wood.
Uses Both the shaft and grip of a handle can be made of wood. Rake heads are also sometimes wooden.
Pros Pleasant to hold, with a warm feel in cold weather. Wooden shafts cause less vibration than fibreglass or metal shafts, making them more comfortable to use. A wooden shaft is easier to replace if it breaks.
Cons Wood is a natural material, so handles may vary in quality and strength – if a shaft has a weak point, it will break when used as a lever.

FIBREGLASS
Made by bonding fine matted glass fibres with a synthetic resin.
Uses Shafts of long-handled tools.
Pros Lightweight, yet 20–30 per cent stronger than a hardwood shaft.
Cons Fibreglass handles transmit vibrations from the shaft to your arms, so they can be tiring to use.

PLASTIC
Plastic once had a poor reputation for durability. If tools were left in sunlight for long periods, ultraviolet light made the plastic brittle. Better-quality plastics such as polypropylene are worth seeking out.
Uses D grips on spade and fork handles. Plastic coating on metal or wooden shafts. Grips on the ends of hoes, rakes and smaller hand tools. Handles of pruners and loppers are often plastic or plastic-coated. Sometimes used for tool heads such as leaf rakes.
Pros Inexpensive and can be moulded to suit the contours of the hand. Easy to wipe clean. Lighter than wood, so useful for long-handled tools.
Cons Plastic coating often splits in time. Can become brittle if left in sunlight, but good-quality plastic is long-lasting. Rough mouldings can be uncomfortable.

HOW METAL TOOL HEADS ARE MADE
A mixture of iron and carbon (sometimes with additives such as manganese or chromium) is heated to a high temperature and cooled. More expensive tools may be described as 'hardened and tempered', which means the metal has been reheated at a lower temperature to mix the elements together. Hardening and tempering make the tool stronger and more malleable.

A tool head made from a single piece of forged metal is stronger and better balanced than one that is pressed out of a sheet of metal. During the forging process, the metal is heated and rolled over blocks. This working and shaping creates a head that is thicker where it will be subjected to pressure, yet thinner where a cutting edge is needed. Tool heads that are stamped or pressed from a sheet of carbon steel, then bent into shape, are cheaper to make, but weaker than forged tools. A tool made by welding several pieces of metal together, which is easy to spot, will have a potential weakness at the point of

cultivating and planti

spades

The aim of digging the soil is to improve its physical structure and promote healthy root growth. Obstacles like rubble and old tree or weed roots can be removed, while at the same time more air spaces are created in the soil and organic matter can be incorporated. A spade slices into the soil, then is lifted to turn the earth. Spades have lots of other uses, from planting trees and shrubs to cutting turf, and most gardeners will need at least one basic tool.

Dimensions vary according to the manufacturer, but for a digging spade, a blade of around 18cm wide and 28cm deep is typical. The depth of the blade is known as the 'spit' and is used as a measure; for example, a head gardener might instruct his team to dig to one spit deep or, to make their lives even harder, two spits. The simplest way to dig a small area is to take a spade full of soil (i.e. one spit deep), lift the blade and turn it over so the soil is put back upside down, then chop the soil several times with the sharp edge of the blade. To dig a larger area, particularly one that has never been cultivated, it is best to use a more systematic method called 'single digging' (see page 16).

If the edge of the blade is kept sharp, a spade can be used to cut turf, skim off weeds or cut through small roots. Smaller, shorter border spades (see page 30) are designed for planting in confined areas. Being lighter, they also make good digging tools for those who find full-sized spades daunting.

Choosing spades For digging and for levering out established plants, choose a tool with a forged head. The parts under stress are made thicker to strengthen them, and the blade edge, which needs to be sharp, is rolled thinner. Stainless-steel heads are easier to dig with than carbon-steel ones as the soil does not cling to them as much; neither do they rust. The weakest point is where the shaft of the handle joins the head: if you want a tool for heavy work, look for one with a solid socket or strapped head (see 'Spade speak' below).

To find a tool you feel comfortable with, go through the actions of using it in the shop. Handle length is critical: it should be long enough to enable you to keep your back straight at all times. Even if you are of medium height, you might prefer a handle longer than the average 70–75cm. On the other hand, if you need a shorter tool, consider a border version. The lengths given in the captions refer to the combined measurements of the shaft and the grip. The choice of material for the shaft and grip is mostly down to personal preference, although each has its pros and cons (see page 10). Check that the top of the blade is wide enough for your foot; try tools with and without a tread to rest your foot on. Although it is usually more comfortable, a tread adds to the weight, and you might prefer to use a plastic attachment instead.

Spade speak

O **Grip** The handle attached to the end of the shaft. There are several types: a T grip, made of wood or polypropylene, is a horizontal handle at right angles to the shaft. It does not enclose the hand, so it suits people with large hands or who like to wear gloves while digging. It is easy to push down against a T grip, but twisting actions are difficult. A YD grip, which is also known as a 'wishbone handle', is made by splitting a shaft made of a wood such as hickory or ash and steaming it into a Y shape, then fitting a piece of wood to the end; nowadays the end can also be metal or polypropylene. It is an expensive process, so expect to pay more for this type of handle. A D grip is a polypropylene

handle fixed to the end of the shaft. As it is made in a mould, it can be shaped for comfort. Both D and YD grips are good for twisting actions.

O **Shaft** The straight part of the handle that extends from the grip down to the tool head. Shafts can be made of hardwood, fibreglass or metal. The section of a metal shaft that might be held while levering soil is often covered by a polypropylene grip that extends halfway down the shaft.

O **Socket** The part of the tool head that attaches to the shaft. The strength of the socket will determine how strong the tool will be during levering actions. An open socket is made by bending a flat piece of metal round the shaft without completely enclosing it.

These are found on less expensive tools and are not as strong as solid sockets and strapped heads, both of which are made from a single piece of forged metal. A solid socket completely encloses the end of the shaft. Strapped tools have metal straps that extend a long way up the shaft and are secured with industrial rivets. The latter is the strongest method of attachment, but it adds weight to the tool. If a wooden shaft breaks, a spade with a socket is easier to repair than one with straps.

O **Tread** The part of the blade where you put your foot while digging is bent over slightly to provide a platform. It makes digging more comfortable on the feet and protects footwear.

1 Traditional spade With a wooden shaft split and steamed to form a YD handle, and a forged carbon-steel head, this digging spade has the appearance of a tool of yesteryear. In fact, it is one of a new range of tools with a traditional design. If you like the look and feel of wood and are prepared to clean and sharpen the blade, you could end up with a tool to pass on to the next generation; this one came with a 25-year guarantee. The handle length is 73cm.

4 Modern long-handled spade A 108cm-long handle and an angled shaft of tubular steel should help medium-height and even tall gardeners keep their backs straight while digging. The shaft is topped with an angled polypropylene D grip. The forged-steel head features a built-in tread.

5 Draining spade As its name suggests, this spade is designed for digging drains and channels in very wet soils. The stainless-steel blade is long yet narrow and is slightly dished. This example was hand-forged in the Netherlands, but similar-shaped spades were once traditional in Ireland and in northern England. A wooden shaft and T grip make up the handle, which is 85cm long.

6 The Bigfoot This deceptively simple plastic device can be slotted over the top of a blade without a tread to provide a more comfortable platform for your foot while digging. It is suitable for blades up to about 19cm wide.

2 Stainless-steel spade A digging spade with a stainless-steel head cuts through the earth easily with a minimal amount of soil adhering to the blade. It will stay shiny even if you forget to clean it. This model has an extra-long socket for added strength. The wooden shaft is topped with an angled polypropylene D grip, and the handle length is 73cm.

3 Traditional long-handled spade This spade's extra-long wooden shaft helps taller gardeners to keep their back straight while digging, and it gives extra leverage. With a plain handle like this, there is no risk of your hand being pinched or confined. For more comfortable digging, your foot sits on a tread welded to the top of the manganese-steel blade. The handle length is 128cm.

1   2   3   4   5

6

forks

Like spades, forks are used to improve the structure of the soil. With their four pointed tines, they penetrate stony or compacted ground more easily than a spade, but they bring less soil to the surface. Once the soil has been turned, the back of the fork can be used to break up clods. As well as being easier to use on hard or stony ground, forks are more efficient than spades when digging heavy soils, as clay doesn't stick to the tines as it does to a solid blade. A fork is also better for clearing perennial weed roots. Forks can be used to turn compost and aerate lawns, and a pair of forks placed back to back is ideal for dividing large clumps of fibrous-rooted perennials.

Forks are similar in construction to spades, and the same considerations regarding materials, joints, handle lengths and grips apply when choosing them (see page 12). Again, it is important to try a fork in the shop before buying, to ensure that it is comfortable to hold and that the handle is the correct length for your height.

1 Border fork Made of the same materials as the garden fork, but with a narrower head, this stainless-steel fork is lighter and less tiring to use. It is also easier to wield in densely planted beds and borders. Border maintenance tasks such as digging out weeds, forking in soil improvers and lifting perennials for division can all be done with this one tool. The handle length is 73cm.

2 Stainless-steel garden fork Stainless steel is a popular material for digging forks as it moves easily through the soil and will not rust. This inexpensive model has a metal shaft and a polypropylene grip. The handle length is 73cm. Forks are also useful for lifting large- to medium-sized plants out of the ground and moving materials such as garden compost from a wheelbarrow to the soil.

3 Manure or dung fork The curved tines of this fork are designed for lifting and scooping manure or compost. These are not heavy-duty tools, so choose a lightweight version if you are of slight build. This example is made of stainless steel with a wooden shaft and a T grip. The handle length is 93cm.

4 Potato fork The tines of a potato fork are broad and flat with dull ends so you can lift up the earth without spearing your crop. It is useful for harvesting other root crops, too. The handle length is 73cm.

5 Spork Sharp, narrow blades between the tines gives this tool the ease of forking and the cutting edge of a spade. It is not a serious substitute for a separate spade and fork, but is useful for routine border maintenance, such as light digging, for example to clear a small area for planting, getting rid of small roots and scraping off weeds on the soil surface. The tool shown here is a stainless-steel border spork with a plastic-coated metal shaft. The handle length is 73cm.

other digging tools

There are several other tools for cultivating the soil. Round-point shovels, heavy-duty hoes and mattock-picks can be used for excavating channels, unearthing rocks and digging. Heavy-duty hoes are traditional in hot regions such as Africa and parts of southern Europe, where they come into their own for working dry or stony soils or land choked with weed roots. Mattocks and picks tend to be used more as ground-clearing tools, and a mattock-pick has both heads on one tool.

Heavy-duty hoes and mattock-picks are known as 'eye' tools as their weighty carbon-steel heads have a hole or 'eye' to take the wooden handle. They can be bought with the handle attached or as separate items. Tool heads are sold by weight – usually around 1kg. Handles are made of ash or hickory and are typically 1–1.2m in length. The heads need to be fitted tightly or they could fly off.

A good-quality shovel made from a single piece of forged carbon steel with a closed socket is ideal for heavy digging. It is more expensive than a pressed- or stamped-steel version, but will last longer and feel better balanced. Shovels with wooden shafts and plain handles enable your hands to move along the shaft easily, although T, YD and D grips are available. Round-point shovels have longer handles than spades or forks, making it easier for taller gardeners to keep a straight back while digging.

1 Round-point shovel With its pointed, tapering blade, this shovel is easy to push into the soil. The 123cm-long wooden handle and slight lift on the blade mean you can keep your back straight while levering the soil up. This tool can also be used for planting trees, shrubs and large perennials, carrying loose materials and cutting tree roots. The blade is carbon steel.

2 Square-point shovel The blade of this shovel has steep sides, a high lift, and a flat edge at the end, making it ideal for carrying loose material. It is also useful for adding topsoil or grit to a border. As the head is made of pressed steel and has an open socket, it can cope with light digging only. The handle length is 70cm.

3 Mattock-pick A mattock-pick is swung over the head, and the heavy tool head is brought down to break up the ground, so it is not for the faint-hearted. This is two tools in one, with a pick for deep digging or making narrow, deep trenches for cables or irrigation, and a mattock for chopping roots and ground clearing.

4 Heavy-duty hoe Made of forged carbon steel, this hoe's head weighs 0.8kg – about the right weight for heavy digging if you are strong and able. Those of a slight build may prefer a lighter version at 0.6kg. Heavy-duty hoes use the weight of the head to bite into the ground, but unlike mattock-picks, are lifted only to eye or shoulder level.

5 Duck-foot digger This multipurpose tool is lighter than a spade, but more versatile than a digging hoe. The triangular, carbon-steel head has a pointed end to break up hard, stony ground, while the curved edge can scoop out holes and chop through roots. The zigzag edge is for weeding and raking. An extra-long wooden handle (1.5m) keeps your back straight.

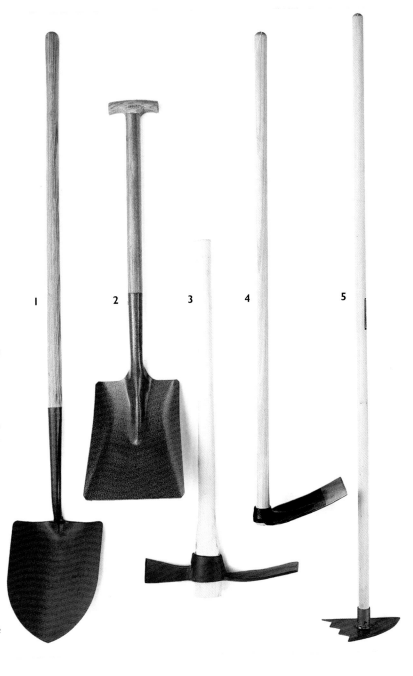

1 2 3 4 5

Single digging

The purpose of single digging is to get the soil into the ideal condition for root growth by clearing any obstacles and opening up compacted soil. Digging incorporates more air spaces in between the mineral particles (clay or sand, for example) of the soil. It is also an opportunity for adding organic matter to improve the soil structure. Well-rotted material such as garden compost provides food for microorganisms, which break it down to form humus. The humus coats the mineral particles of the soil and prevents it from becoming waterlogged, making it easier to cultivate.

When single digging, it is important to dig only the top fertile layer (topsoil) and to avoid diluting it with underlying subsoil, which is much less fertile and usually lighter in color. The depth of topsoil varies in different regions; ideally, it is 15–30cm deep, but it can be much shallower.

Avoid digging when the ground is wet and sticky or frozen. The best times to dig are from late autumn to early winter or in early spring.

1 Mark out the area of cleared ground as a square or rectangle and add organic matter over the surface. Divide the area into trenches about 30cm wide and 1.2–1.5m long; this can be done by eye. Dig out the first trench in one corner of the plot by starting 30cm in from one marked edge. Hold the spade by the handle and use your foot to drive the blade straight down into the soil. The aim is to make the trench the same depth as the blade, but you can take several bites out of the soil to reach this depth.

2 Pull back on the spade to loosen the soil. To lift the soil out, bend your knees, slide one hand down the shaft and pull up a spade full of soil. Tip the soil from the first trench into a wheelbarrow or onto a sheet of tarpaulin (it will be needed to fill the last trench). Keep your back as straight as possible while digging and take regular breaks between trenches to avoid back strain.

3 Dig a second trench next to the first one. Dig it in the same way, but this time throw the soil forward to fill in the first trench. The organic matter that was spread on the surface will be mixed in with the soil. Dig a third trench and repeat the process until the whole area has been dug over. Use the soil from the first trench to fill the final trench. A dug-over plot can be left over winter, when the frost and rain will break down the clods of earth.

Working a heavy clay soil

Nori and Sandra Pope began gardening together on Vancouver Island, Canada, where they ran a garden design company and nursery, and took over the management of Hadspen Garden in Somerset in 1987. Since then, their inspirational use of colour in the borders (such as the double yellow border shown opposite) and the kitchen garden has established Hadspen as a rich source of exciting planting ideas, which are documented in their book Colour by Design. Here Sandra describes why they prefer to use shovels instead of spades to work the soil at Hadspen.

'Conventional spades are fine for lifting perennials and cutting turf, but we find that using a spade to dig deeply is like trying to stick a flat plank into the ground. Pointed shovels, on the other hand, work wonders on our heavy clay soil. Such tools are widely used in Canada but not so much in Britain. I use a standard-length shovel with a fairly small head, but Nori is taller (1.8m) and finds a longer-handled shovel helps keep his back straight while digging over the ground in the kitchen garden or planting in the borders. To improve the soil, we cover the surface in autumn with a layer of farmyard muck no less than 15cm deep. When we turn it in early spring, the pointed shovel cuts neatly into the damp, heavy soil. If the earth is well mulched, then every time we plant, a bit more organic matter gets worked into the soil – a double gain.'

turning and levelling

Once the soil has been dug, its surface needs to be prepared for sowing or planting. Rakes, cultivators and some types of hoe all have a part to play. Rakes are used with a push-pull action, whereas cultivators are pulled or dragged through the soil to lift and turn it.

A rake will do a good job of rough levelling and raking soil into a fine, crumb-like tilth in all but the smallest beds. The wider the head, the quicker large areas of ground can be cultivated. Tool heads should be cleaned after use, although this is often tricky with the more elaborate cultivators and tillers. The teeth on many of these tools are sharp, so don't leave them lying around.

Some hoes can also be used for turning and levelling. These include the heavier hoes used with a chopping action to break up the soil surface (see page 15) and the draw hoes, hand hoes and hoes like the ridging hoe (see page 22) that are shaped for earthing up.

1 Basic garden rake This inexpensive tool, with teeth cut from one piece of steel, will cope with a range of soils and is ideal for tamping down earth. The metal handle is telescopic, measuring 88cm when closed and 1.47m when fully extended.

2 Detachable bow rake The bow rake has arms that help to keep the stainless-steel head level as you rake, a useful feature for coping with stony ground. It is quite a wide rake at 35cm, and the 14 teeth are slightly curved, making it less likely to move off course as it is dragged along. For details of interchangeable systems, see page 9.

3 Landscaping rake A special tool for spreading and levelling large areas of topsoil, for example before laying a lawn. The extra-wide (70cm) head and 18 widely spaced teeth mean the task can be done quickly. A wide head puts a strain on the connection between the head and the shaft, so check the tool for extra support. In this model the carbon-steel head is firmly attached to the wooden handle and has a straight back edge for precise levelling. Other designs may have wooden handles with wooden or polypropylene teeth.

4 Add-on handles Fixing extra handles on the shafts of long-handled tools such as rakes, hoes and brooms makes push-pull actions easier, especially if you have back problems or find gripping the shaft painful. One handle is attached to the end of the shaft, and the other lower down at right angles to the first. A single add-on handle can be used on short-handed tools. These handles are plastic with stainless-steel clamps, tightened with a key.

5 Hand rake For creating a fine soil texture over a small area, such as a gap in a border where hardy annuals are to be sown, or for preparing a bed for sowing vegetables in a potager, you will need a hand rake. This stainless-steel version has five teeth on a short wooden handle.

6 Detachable flower rake A small carbon-steel head with five teeth and a working width of 8–9cm makes this flower rake useful for cultivating between established plants. It has an extension handle with an upper limit of 78cm. See page 9 for details of interchangeable systems.

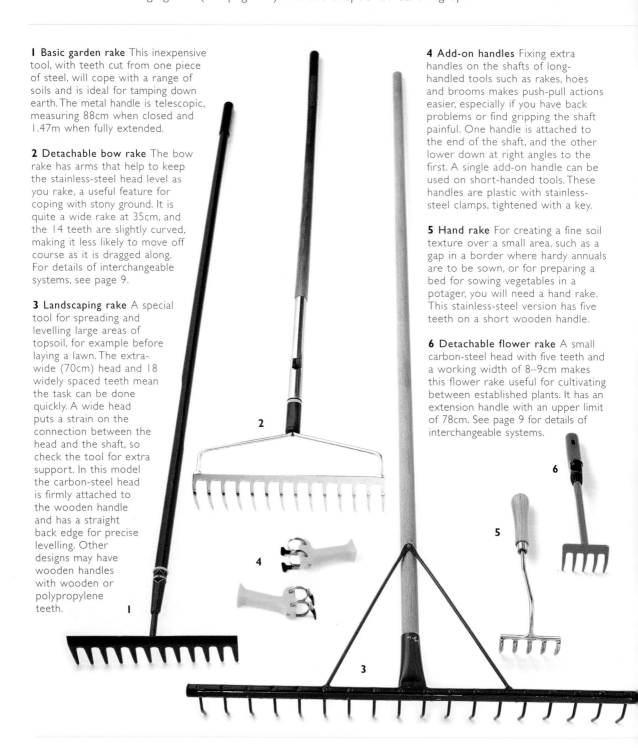

Choosing rakes and cultivators

Lightweight tools are fine for surface cultivation or where the soil is high in organic matter or sandy and so easy to work. The lighter tools have a 'tang and ferrule' joint: a long piece of metal (the tang) extending from the head is pushed into the end of the shaft and held tight by a small metal ring (the ferrule). Tools that are dragged deeply through the earth or used in stony or heavy clay soils need to be robust: look for strapped or full sockets and forged heads with strong teeth, prongs or tines. (See page 12 for an explanation of sockets.)

The teeth on a garden rake are usually 2.5cm apart. A 12-tooth or 30cm rake is about right for most people, but you might prefer a narrower tool head, around 10–15cm, for cultivating between established plants, or an even wider head for levelling large areas.

Long-handled tools reduce the need for bending. They can cover a larger area quickly and are useful for cultivating at the back of a bed or border. Short-handled tools are easier to manoeuvre in small or raised beds and enable you to cultivate between plants. Telescopic or detachable handles of different lengths can be adjusted to suit the needs of different beds or users. Handle lengths are not given for most of the tools featured as they are held along the shaft rather than at the end.

7 Detachable three-pronged cultivator This stainless-steel cultivator is 15cm wide with arrowhead tips for cutting into heavy soils. Forming part of an interchangeable system (see page 9), it is illustrated here with a 135cm handle.

8 Three-pronged cultivator When it is dragged through the soil, this cultivator will pull up weeds and break up compacted ground and 'capped' soil (soil that has been dug and raked to a fine tilth sometimes forms a crust on the surface when it dries out after rain). The middle prong is shorter than the other two and bites into the earth first. The thickness of the prongs and how they are shaped at the ends varies depending on the manufacturer. This one has a 12cm-wide stainless-steel head and an aluminium shaft.

9 Detachable four-star tiller Four star-shaped wheels on this carbon-steel cultivator loosen the soil and help form a crumb-like texture ready for sowing seed. It has a working width of 14cm and a 1.5m handle is recommended. The cultivator performs best on easily worked soil rather than stony or compacted ground, and is quite fiddly to clean. For details of interchangeable systems, see page 9.

10 Manure drag Like a fork with the tines bent to 90 degrees, this tool is used with a dragging movement to shift manure and compost into piles or for removing weeds and debris from ditches. Heavy-duty versions like the one pictured have a solid strapped socket and long handle. A smaller, lighter version can be used to break up compacted ground.

11 Canterbury fork This versatile tool is useful for loosening the surface of soil, weeding and light digging. Either use it with the chopping action of a heavy-duty hoe or drag the tines through soil like a cultivator or rake. The head is made from forged carbon steel and weighs 0.7kg.

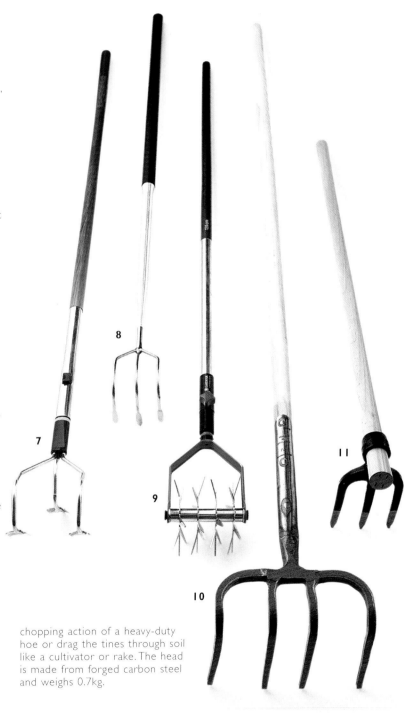

Using a garden rake

Levelling soil Any lumps of soil in ground that has been dug and weeded can be broken up and dispersed with the back of the rake head. Hold the rake so the teeth are pointing upwards, and push the pile of soil over any slight depressions so it is distributed evenly over the bed.

Firming the ground Also known as 'tamping down', firming the ground ensures that the soil particles are making contact with one another and reduces the amount of settling that occurs after soil cultivation. Hold the rake vertically with the teeth parallel to the soil surface and press down gently but firmly.

Preparing a seedbed To create a seedbed for outdoor sowing, the soil needs to be raked into a tilth with fine, even soil particles and a level surface. Move the teeth of the rake backwards and forwards through the soil. Rake in one direction across the bed, then turn and rake at right angles to the first rake marks.

Making a seed drill The corner of a rake head can be used to make a V-shaped seed drill. Mark the position of the row with a garden line or a straight-edged plank of wood. Hold the rake with the teeth uppermost and the corner in the soil, and pull it towards you. The depth of a typical seed drill is about 1.5cm.

The no-dig approach

A rich soil brings a good crop of leafy salads, as shown opposite, but this does not always mean deep, strenuous digging. Mary Moody is one of Australia's best-known gardening authors and broadcasters, with a keen interest in organic growing. Here she reveals how she has built up the fertility in her own kitchen garden with the aid of a hoe, a rake and worms.

'I believe that layering organic materials on the soil surface and letting the worms drag them down into the soil is more effective than deep cultivation. I use straw, newspaper and manure from my chickens as surface mulch, and only cultivate the rows where the seeds are to be planted. Using a long-handled hoe with a heavy, sharp end, I just turn over the top layer of soil and remove the weeds, before raking smooth the soil surface. Digging deeply would disturb the worms. I have worked for 20 years to build the fertility in my garden on what was originally very poor sandy soil. From having less than 5cm of topsoil when I arrived, I now have around 45cm.'

hoeing

Most of the hoes featured here are designed to remove weed seedlings either before or after sowing or planting. If you hoe little and often during the growing season, you will need to use less chemical weedkiller, or even none at all, which will both save you money and help protect the environment.

These tools are used near the soil surface to cut or sever the young weed stems without disturbing the roots of cultivated plants. Hoes have one or more blades, but the angle and shape vary greatly. Long-handled hoes are used with both hands on the shaft. Short-handled versions are used one-handed while squatting or kneeling; use your free hand to pick up debris or hold plants back from the blade.

Choosing hoes If you have a lot of ground to cover, a long-handled hoe will weed it faster than a short-handled model. As it is used from a standing position, it is the best choice for anyone who suffers with back pain or knee problems. Check the feel and length of the shaft before you buy; most have plain handles, but some have a cushioned grip. Short-handled hoes are easier to manoeuvre in densely planted areas with less risk of disturbing growing plants. Where the tool head is joined to the shaft is a potential weak point. In some hoes the head is attached by a socket or eye joint or a detachable fitting, but most have a tang-and-ferrule attachment (see page 19), which is strong enough to cope with surface cultivation and makes the tools light to hold.

You will need at least one hoe to deal with weed seedlings. Keen gardeners who make a lot of outdoor sowings or grow vegetables will probably want an additional hoe for making seedbeds or earthing up.

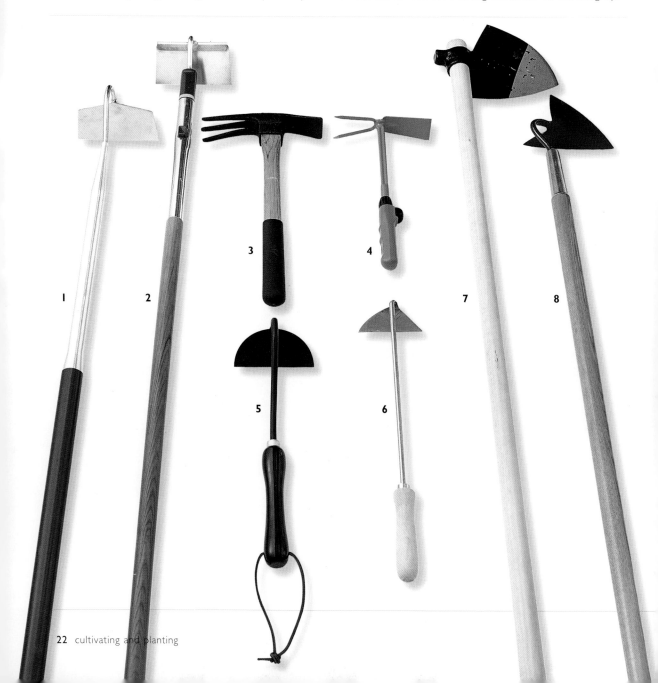

1   2   3   4   7   8

5   6

1 Basic draw hoe A draw hoe is used to chop at weeds. It copes well with hard ground and can also be used for earthing up vegetables and making broad, shallow trenches, for example for sowing peas. This one has a 15cm-wide stainless-steel blade and an aluminium shaft.

2 Detachable draw hoe The head of this draw hoe can be slotted into handles of different lengths. Made of stainless steel, the head is 15cm wide and has a swan-necked arm that tilts the blade at a sharp angle towards the user so it chops or slices weeds just below the soil surface. This makes the hoe harder to use for earthing up. A smaller 10cm head is available. For details of interchangeable systems, see page 9.

3 Three-pronged hand hoe A style of hoe that has been used for centuries throughout the world. This modern-day version has a head that is ready-fitted to a shaped wooden handle with a cushioned grip. The head weighs 0.5kg, and the chopping end is around 5cm wide.

4 Detachable two-pronged hand hoe Part of an interchangeable system (see page 9), this lightweight hand hoe is ideal for weeding and cultivating in confined spaces. The straight blade has a working width of 5cm. Other versions – with three prongs or with a heart-shaped blade – are available.

5 Onion hoe These hoes were originally developed for weeding between rows of young onion plants, which are sensitive to competition from weeds. However, they soon proved invaluable for hoeing between rows of any young plant. The flat edge of the blade can be used to scrape out or chop at weeds, and the sharp corners will extract weed roots. This hoe has a wooden handle, and a carbon-steel blade 13cm wide; narrower blades are available.

6 Angle weeder Like the onion hoe, an angle weeder is ideal for working between rows, but is also versatile enough to use around existing plants, as the stainless-steel blade is angled more to the left. The tool shown has a 10cm blade and is designed for right-handers; wider blades and left-handed versions – where the blade is angled to the right – are available.

7 Ridging hoe The pointed carbon-steel blade is designed for preparing seedbeds and earthing up, but this hoe is sturdy enough to be used for extracting the roots of perennial weeds and digging as well. Several sizes of tool head are available, ranging from 0.7 to 1.2kg.

8 Warren hoe A specialized hoe for those who do a lot of sowing in long rows. The triangular carbon-steel head is ideal for drawing out seed drills. The other side of the head is useful for covering the seed with soil. There is no sharp cutting edge, so nearby plants are less likely to be damaged.

9 Dutch hoe A traditional hoe with a single, upward-facing blade that slices through weed seedlings. Used with a push-pull action on or just below the soil surface, it works best on a fine tilth. This one has a 13cm-wide carbon-steel head, which is easy to sharpen, and a metal handle.

10 Swoe Developed in the 1960s as an advance on the Dutch hoe, the swoe has three cutting edges around a head shaped like a number 7. The angle of the head and blades make it ideal for weeding around established plants; it can also go deeper into the ground than many surface hoes. The head is 13cm wide and made of stainless steel. The handle is aluminium.

11 Winged weeder Each side of this push-pull hoe has a sharp edge so it can cut surface weeds in double-quick time. The flat head makes it good for hoeing under established shrubs or fences. The head is carbon steel, and the handle is hardwood. Illustrated here is the 5cm blade with a 130cm handle; it is also available with a short 25cm handle. A larger model has a 21cm blade on a 130cm handle.

12 Oscillating hoe The blade of this hoe has two cutting edges and is attached to the carbon-steel head by a hinge so it cuts on both the push and the pull stroke. The hinge needs to be oiled occasionally. The Swiss Real brand featured here is recommended as the blades can be replaced when they wear out. The blades are supplied as heads only so you need to fix on your own handle. Shown here is the 12cm-wide head; 5cm and 18cm versions are also available.

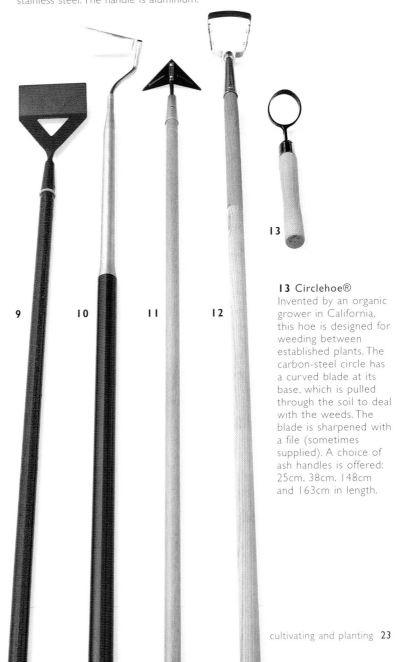

9 10 11 12 13

13 Circlehoe® Invented by an organic grower in California, this hoe is designed for weeding between established plants. The carbon-steel circle has a curved blade at its base, which is pulled through the soil to deal with the weeds. The blade is sharpened with a file (sometimes supplied). A choice of ash handles is offered: 25cm, 38cm, 148cm and 163cm in length.

Using hoes

1 Dutch hoe This traditional tool will tackle a flush of weed seedlings in cultivated or prepared beds. Push the blade forwards so it skims at soil level or just under the surface of the soil, severing the weeds from their roots, then pull back. Work backwards as you hoe to avoid compacting the hoed ground and treading weed seedlings back into it. Keep the blade sharp by filing it.

2 Onion hoe This small, short-handled hoe gives good control when weeding between rows of closely growing plants, such as onions or hardy annuals sown directly into the ground. Use it with a chopping action as you would a draw hoe.

3 Draw hoe Chopping weeds is one of many uses of a draw hoe. Raise the hoe above the ground and push it down to strike the side of the weed and sever it from its roots. A draw hoe quickly clears weeds from beds or borders before planting or sowing, and copes with older, tougher annual weeds better than a Dutch hoe.

Weeding a gravel garden

Beth Chatto is an influential plantswoman and author who over 40 years has transformed several acres of wasteland near Colchester in Essex into the world-famous Beth Chatto Gardens and nursery. These are a mecca for anyone interested in growing and combining perennial plants in the toughest of conditions. In 1991 she created the Gravel Garden (see opposite), planting drought-tolerant perennials in a third of a hectare of poor, gravelly soil on the site of a former car park. This is a living experiment to create a decorative garden that requires no watering, even in times of drought. Here she explains how the Gravel Garden is weeded and describes her favourite weeding tools.

'My preferred method of weed control in established beds and borders is mulching, particularly where the soil is dry, but hoeing is invaluable for dealing with the crops of weed seedlings that arise when the soil has been disturbed. We did not apply a mulch in the Gravel Garden in the first year. Instead, the weed seedlings were hoed away with swoes, and there was no need for chemical weed control. My favourite hoes are those that can be used without damaging the recently planted perennials. The long-handled Wilkinson Sword swoe is a hoe I have used for many years (see above, where it is shown weeding around a young sedum plant). It cuts through the soil with an easy push-pull action. For closer work, I like to use a short-handled onion hoe, which allows you to work around small plants.'

other hand weeders

While hoes cope well with weed seedlings, specialized hand weeders are useful for dealing with isolated, deep-rooted problem plants or for working in tricky places like rockeries or ponds. There are devices here to help you extract all sorts of weeds, but like the majority of weeding tools, they are most effective on young plants.

Choosing hand weeders Hand weeders are very diverse. Short-handled tools are designed to be used when kneeling or squatting. While working in this position, it is useful to have one tool that can not only weed but double up as a tool for the next task. For example, a weeding knife will also make small planting holes; other weeding tools can also be used to make seed drills. Tools for extracting isolated weeds include hand forks and their variations. For gardeners who prefer to weed standing up, there are a number of ingenious long-handled weeders.

Most gardeners will find at least one of the following useful: a weeding knife, a hand weeder that can be used to make seed drills, and a weeding fork. For prizing weeds out of a heavy soil, look for hand weeders with forged metal heads; for weeding in a light soil, you will get by with pressed or stamped versions. In most cases the tool heads are attached to the handles by a tang-and-ferrule joint (see page 19); these vary in quality, and the heads may fall off in time as wood around the metal spike rots. Hand weeders are generally inexpensive and are often replaced rather than repaired.

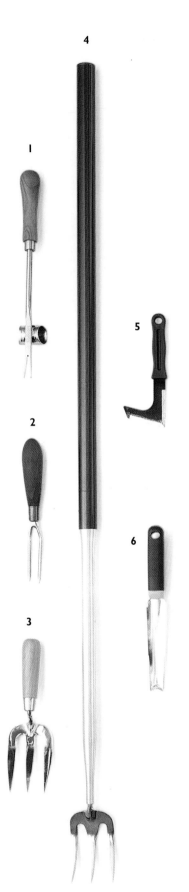

4

1

5

2

6

3

1 Taproot weeder Also known as a daisy grubber or lawn weeder, this tool extracts weeds with taproots without greatly disturbing the soil. It will deal with dandelions, thistles and daisies, and is invaluable for lawn and gravel gardens. The simplest versions are forked tools about 25cm long with a bend in the blade that acts as a fulcrum. Shown here is a more advanced version with extra leverage provided by a bigger fulcrum and a longer handle. It is made from hand-forged stainless steel with a wooden handle. To use it, insert the fork around the base of the plant with the fulcrum on the ground. Then press down on the handle to prize the weed out with the roots.

2 Weeding fork Sometimes called the 'Jekyll weeder', this was a favourite tool of garden designer Gertrude Jekyll. Having only two prongs, it is more precise than a conventional hand fork for removing weeds from amongst other plants. The head is made of stainless steel and is joined to a wooden handle with a brass ferrule. This model is a well-balanced tool that is comfortable to use.

3 Hand fork These three-tined forks are designed for digging to a depth of up to 10cm in cultivated soil and easing out young perennial weeds, root and all. They can also be used to lightly fork over cultivated beds

after adding fertilizer. The cheapest models are moulded from one piece of plastic or metal, while others have metal heads and handles of wood, metal or plastic. With a stainless-steel head and a wooden handle, this one is a comfortable, easy-care tool in the mid-price range.

4 Long-handled hand fork The long-handled version of a hand fork was designed for weeding or forking over border soil while standing, but it is also useful for reaching further back into borders without disturbing other plants. This one is made of stainless steel with an aluminium shaft.

5 Paving weeder This inexpensive weeder is a knife whose blade is slim enough to slip between cracks in paving. Hold it as you would a breadknife, pressing down and sawing to cut the weeds. Then use the hooked end to pull them out. Weeding large areas may be tiring, but it's better for the environment than a path weedkiller. This tool has a metal blade and a plastic handle.

6 Weeding knife The narrow yet deep blade is perfect for removing deep-rooted weeds with minimum soil disturbance, and is invaluable for lawns, rockeries or containers. It is also useful for planting small bulbs or transplants. The blade is made of carbon steel, and the handle is plastic.

7 Pointing trowel This small trowel is actually designed for pointing brickwork or for archaeology field work, but it also makes a precise yet lightweight weeding tool. The pointed end can get into the tiniest space to winkle out weeds, or it can make a short seed drill. Use the edge of the blade to skim the soil surface or the whole blade as a trowel for planting small plants if the soil has been well cultivated. This one has a 13cm-long carbon-steel blade and a wooden handle. Sizes vary.

8 Ibis With its curved head ending in a sharp point, this Oriental tool is incredibly versatile. Use it to dig deep down and extract weeds or to make a seed drill. The main body of the head is large enough to scoop out soil for planting, or the blade can be used like a hoe. An ibis is a useful item for a vegetable plot, especially one with raised beds where long-handled weeders are unwieldy. The head is forged carbon steel and is attached to a wooden handle.

9 Core weeder This long-handled weeder is used from a standing position, and it extracts the weed with a neat core of earth containing the roots. It is therefore useful for perennial weeds and works best with clump-forming or rosette-type species such as dandelions. It has a tubular steel shaft with plastic handles and a foot rest. Store it somewhere dry to prevent the spring mechanism rusting.

10 Spot weeder Spot treatment of weeds uses less weedkiller than blanket spraying, and this device offers an economical alternative to buying ready-to-use spot weeders. Another bonus is you can apply the weedkiller from a standing position. The chemical is mixed and diluted in a plastic tube. To treat a weed, simply push down on the top. This action presses a sponge onto the weed, and a small amount of weedkiller is released. After use, dunk the sponge head in clean water several times. The sponge head will need replacing after a while (a spare is included).

11 Pond net A net with 3mm mesh will remove floating vegetation from a pond, but to collect algae you need a net with closed mesh gauze. The version shown here is a small algae net with a fixed, 113cm, anodized-aluminium handle. Larger nets with telescopic handles for larger ponds are available.

12 Pond weeder To pull out the thin strings of blanket weed from between other floating pond plants, dip the metal end of the weeder in the water. Rotate the shaft of the tool by hand to gather up the weed. Once you have gathered enough, swing the tool so the weed is held over the bank and pull the plastic end of the handle. This retracts the metal end holding the weed inside the hollow shaft, and the blanket weed falls off without your having to touch it.

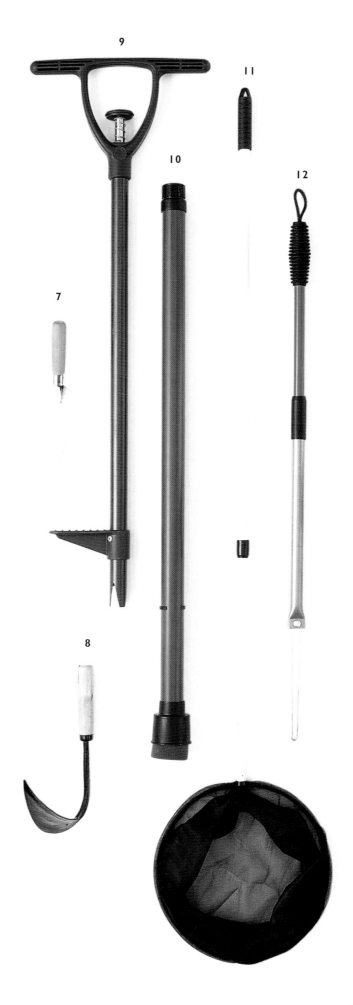

Using weeding tools

Weeding a lawn A few rosette-type lawn weeds such as plantains can be removed, root and all, with a core weeder. The tool is placed over the weed, and a core of earth containing the weed and root is removed by twisting the handle. A knob releases the weed.

Weeding between plants Place the prongs of a weeding fork around the crown of the weed and ease it out of the soil, root and all. This tool allows discrete weeding in the tightest spaces, even a rockery, with minimum disturbance to surrounding plants.

Weeding between paving To cut through weeds growing between paving slabs, use the blade on the outside of a paving weeder, pushing it down as far as possible. Then turn the knife over and hook out as much of the weeds and their roots as possible.

Weeding and planting A tool that can do more than one job is a boon when you are short of time. An ibis cultivator copes with hoeing, digging out perennial weeds, chopping up soil and making planting holes. It is useful when you need to weed then plant straightaway.

Weeding ponds

Anthony Archer-Wills has designed and built thousands of water features in both Europe and the USA, including the pond at Stile House in West Sussex (shown opposite). In addition, he advises owners of both small ponds and vast lakes on how to care for them. Here he gives some practical tips on removing weeds and other debris from ponds.

'Blanketweed is a very invasive algae that multiplies rapidly in nutrient-rich water in warm, sunny conditions. The long strings get tangled around plants and eventually mat together like a fabric. To remove them, use a stick-like tool such as a bamboo cane or a pond weeder and twirl it around in the water. This will gently draw out the strings of weed from around other plants. Lift out the blanketweed before it gets wound up too tight and leave it on the pond edge for a day or so to allow trapped pond creatures to crawl back to the water. A lawn rake can be used to pull out sheets of blanketweed covering a large pond, but make sure you do not drag out any floating plants. Another versatile tool is a pressure nozzle on the end of a hose, preferably one that can be adjusted to give either a wide spray or a jet of water. Use the spray to shepherd excess duckweed to one part of the pond and scoop it out with a pond net. Use the jet to dislodge beetles and aphids from waterlilies into the water, where they will be eaten by fish. On hot summer nights, a powerful jet directed at the surface of a pond will supply a quick shot of oxygen to the water and give flagging fish a boost.

In autumn, clear excessive plant debris from the margins of the pond, although any reeds or grasses can be left for winter interest and to provide cover for amphibians. I prefer to wade into the water and remove vegetation gently so as not to harm fish. I either pull out debris by hand or cut the vegetation with a sickle.'

planting spades and trowels

Plants with large roots such as trees, shrubs, climbers and sizeable perennials need large planting holes, which are best dug with a long-handled tool like a border spade. This has a slightly smaller blade than a standard garden spade, making it lighter and easier to use in confined spaces. A typical blade is 23cm long and 14cm wide, which is big enough for digging and making planting holes, yet easy to manoeuvre in well-stocked borders.

Another option is to use a planting spade. This is a halfway house between a round-point shovel and a trowel, and is even easier to use than a border spade when working in a plant-packed border or a small bed. Spades (and shovels) are also useful for making V-shaped slits in the ground to take bare-rooted plants or bulbs. Most gardeners will need at least one tool for digging larger holes.

A trowel is an essential tool for planting out small plants and bulbs. The dished blade, with its rounded point, is light enough to be used with one hand, while the other hand holds the plant.

When planting pot-grown plants with a rootball, use the trowel as a scoop to make a hole. The pointed tip can be used to ladle soil back in around the roots, and the back of the blade to firm the soil down. For small bare-rooted plants or bulbs, it is often quicker to make slits in the earth by holding the trowel like a dagger, with the curve of the blade facing you, and plunging it into the soil. Move it backwards and forwards to make the slit, then simply drop the plant in, remove the trowel and firm down the surrounding soil.

Trowels often have measurements, typically in stages up to 10cm, etched onto the blade: these can be used as a guide when spacing plants as well as to measure the planting depth.

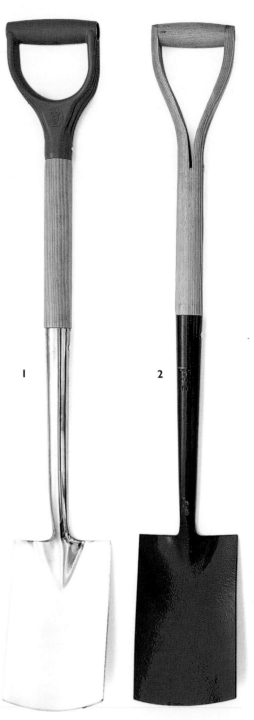

1

2

1 Modern border spade Typical of modern-day tools, this spade has a stainless-steel head and a wooden shaft topped with a D grip of moulded polypropylene. These features make the tool easy to care for, and the long socket provides extra strength. Although this spade is designed for excavating planting holes, gardeners with a small build may find it less tiring to use for more sustained digging than a standard digging spade.

2 Traditional border spade The traditional version has a blade of forged carbon steel and a solid socket around a wooden shaft that is topped with a wooden YD handle. As with the modern border spade, people with a small build may find it easier to use this tool for bigger tasks than a standard digging spade.

3 Planting spade A giant trowel or a miniature spade? In fact, it's a useful tool for gardeners who want to squeeze more plants into packed borders or who grow lots of perennials or herbs. The T grip allows you to push down hard, and the point of the blade means you can dig with great precision. Tall gardeners with large hands and feet may find it difficult to use. This one has a stainless-steel head and a varnished hardwood handle.

Choosing spades and trowels

These are tools that are in use all year round, so it pays to buy good-quality ones that are forged from a single piece of metal. Stainless steel is by far the most popular material as the blades stay shiny and glide easily through the soil. Inexpensive trowels and spades may be fine for light planting into soft, fluffy soil or compost, but when used to prize up stony or compacted soil, they are likely to break where the head meets the handle.

Before buying, hold the tool to check that the balance between blade and handle feels right and that the handle length and the grip are comfortable. Spade handles should be long enough for you to be able to keep your back straight. The average length of 71cm should be the right height for gardeners of small build to plant and dig comfortably; anyone of medium height and even taller gardeners should be fine using a border spade for a short time, but longer spells of digging could lead to backache. Although there is a choice of materials for handles, most people prefer wood for its warmth and the way it wears to the user's hand.

The length of trowel blades is fairly standard at 13–15cm, and the total length of a trowel rarely exceeds 30cm. However, the width of the blade does vary, which affects how easy it is to use. The wider the blade, the more soil it can scoop out, but the weight of the blade can strain the wrists. Wide blades are also rather unwieldy for working amongst established plants. Narrow trowels are lighter and so easier for gardeners with small hands. They are often called bulb-planting trowels, weeding trowels, rockery trowels or transplanting trowels; most can be used for all four purposes. Other options for gardeners with weak wrists or small hands include trowels with handles at a right angle to the blade, or planting spades.

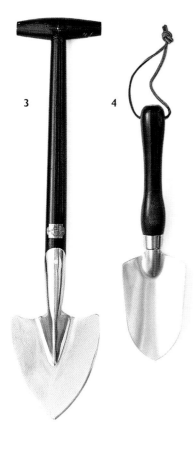

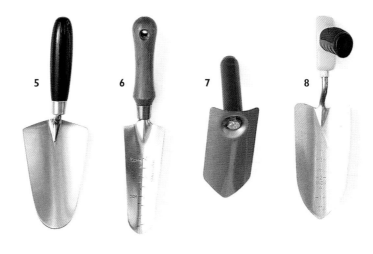

4 Long-handled trowel A familiar stainless-steel trowel for planting out small plants. The long handle makes it particularly useful for someone with large hands. This is one of many trowels in a range that includes even longer-handled versions, narrow-width models and standard- and narrow-width versions in carbon steel. All come with wooden handles and a loop at the end for hanging them up.

5 Standard-width trowel This is a high-quality trowel that comes in a presentation box or as part of a boxed set. The stainless-steel blade has a good cutting edge for penetrating the soil, and is deeply dished so it scoops out enough soil to make a generous planting hole. A brass collar holds the swan-necked tang to the wooden handle.

6 Narrow-width trowel An inexpensive yet versatile trowel with a pointed stainless-steel head and a plastic handle. The narrow blade has planting depths etched on it and is designed for planting bulbs at their correct depth. The blade shape is invaluable for making neat holes in very tight spaces, for example when planting a container or when transplanting young plants from a densely packed seedbed.

7 Right-angled trowel Using a trowel with a downward action to bite into the soil, then pulling it towards you is easier on the wrist and quicker than scooping out soil with a traditional trowel. Therefore, if you have a lot of young plants or bulbs to plant out, a right-angle trowel could be just what you need. The stainless-steel blade is bolted onto a metal handle.

8 Fist-grip trowel This trowel is used with a scoop action, but the handle is at a right angle to the blade to reduce strain on the wrist. The blade is stainless steel, and the handle is plastic with a soft, flexible, rubber grip.

Planting in small spaces

Where there is very little space to make planting holes, use a narrow-width trowel, pointing trowel or dibber. As the holes will not be large enough to add organic material, water the plants well both before and after planting to ensure the compost inside the rootball is moist. Here packs of autumn-flowering cyclamen are used to underplant a small tree in a container.

1 Place the plants in a tray of water for 20 minutes or so before planting. Cyclamen are best watered from underneath as watering from above can encourage grey rot (botrytis).

2 Remove the plants from their packs and space them out on the ground to form an informal drift.

3 Use a narrow-width trowel to make holes slightly bigger than the rootballs. If scooping the soil is tricky, try holding the trowel like a dagger. Plant the cyclamen and firm them in gently with your fingers.

Circular grove

Ivan Hicks is a garden designer who has a knack of taking familiar plants and planting or training them in new and imaginative ways. One of his ideas is a circular grove of young trees that, when grown, are tied together at the top to form a living grotto or, as he also calls it, an 'anti-stress chamber' (the example shown opposite uses the birch Betula jacquemontii). Here Ivan describes how to plant it.

'I often create this feature in clients' lawns and the ideal tool for cutting turf and planting is a border spade – it is more precise than a normal spade and makes less mess. If the grove is small, I take up the turf within the circle and replace it with a geotextile membrane covered with gravel or bark chips.

Six trees planted in a circle measuring 1.2m in diameter is about the minimum size, which would suit an area of lawn measuring 3m by 3m. The circle can be larger to suit the site. Space out the trees evenly, using canes to mark their positions. Leave a gap at least 60cm wide to enter the grove. Dig a hole for each tree, making the hole almost twice the volume of the rootball. Mix half a bucket or so of well-rotted manure with some of the soil, and add to the bottom of the hole. Position the tree in the hole so it is planted to the same depth as it was in its pot, adjusting the level if necessary by adding more or less soil as required. Fill the sides of the hole with soil and firm down with your foot. Tie the leading stems together at the top with garden string. As the trees grow, any vigorous side shoots that threaten to take over from the leading stems can be cut out in midwinter.'

more planting tools

A number of other tools can make planting easier. Dibbers, for example, are useful if you need to plant large numbers of plants in a vegetable plot. Simply push the dibber into the ground to make a planting hole for young transplants.

It is important to match the size of the dibber to the plant. The largest dibbers will make a deep, wide hole; medium-sized dibbers are more versatile, while smaller ones are better for sowing large seeds or small bulbs. (Very small dibbers for pricking out seedlings and cuttings are featured on page 110.) Some models have plain handles, other have grips – try both to see which you prefer. For a large dibber, a T grip is easier to push down into the soil, but a D grip is better for the twisting action to make the hole. For medium to small dibbers, a plain or L-shaped grip is adequate.

Bulb planters are hollow cylinders that take out a core of earth, which is replaced after planting the bulb. Most designs leave a neat hole about 5–8cm in diameter, which is suitable for one tulip or daffodil or two to three smaller bulbs. The advantage of using a bulb planter is that all the bulbs are planted at the same depth, creating an even display, and when you have a large quantity to plant, it's a lot quicker than using a trowel. The only limitation when using a short-handled model is the strength of your wrist.

When buying a bulb planter, check that the handle is comfortable: gardeners with large hands may find that short-handled planters pinch. With long-handled versions, check how easy it is to push down on the handle and to use the foot platform.

Anyone who finds bending or kneeling difficult should seek out long-handled versions of dibbers and bulb planters. Long-handled bulb planters are fairly easy to find, but if you want a really long dibber, you might have to make your own from a long wooden handle.

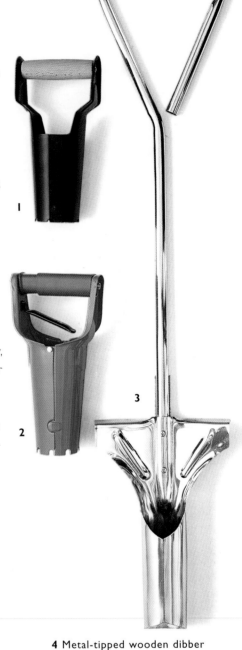

1 Short-handled bulb planter
A basic bulb planter made of painted carbon steel with a typical serrated edge and a horizontal wooden handle. To operate this type of planter, use one hand to push and twist the metal cylinder down to the required depth, then remove it slowly to keep the soil inside. After planting the bulb, release the soil by shaking the planter or turning it upside down.

2 Quick-release bulb planter
The hole is made in the same way as with the short-handled planter, but this model has a lever under the plastic handle that opens the metal sides to release the soil. It works well for dry soil, but in wet conditions the soil clings to the sides of the planter.

3 Long-handled bulb planter
This is an inexpensive bulb planter in chrome-plated steel, but it is effective enough for short-term use. The handle is 65cm long and is bolted to the main body of the planter. It has a metal cylinder, the end of which forms a platform for your foot. It is easy to push the planter through turf and make a hole, but it can be harder to control the planting depth than with a short-handled model. To replace the soil, you'll need to poke it out of the planter with a broom handle. An alternative method is to make all the holes before planting, so the soil is pushed out of the top of the planter by each new core.

4 Metal-tipped wooden dibber
This medium-sized dibber has a point made from coated carbon steel and a wooden handle with a T grip. A sharp metal point is useful for piercing through a sheet mulch to plant potatoes, for example, or to sow large seeds such as sweetcorn.

5 Large wooden dibber
Traditionally, large dibbers were made by sharpening the end of the shaft of a broken spade or fork. This purpose-made wooden one, with a T grip, has a total length of 55cm. Few topsoils are this deep, however, and a typically useful hole would be more like 20–30cm deep, which is ideal for blanching large leeks.

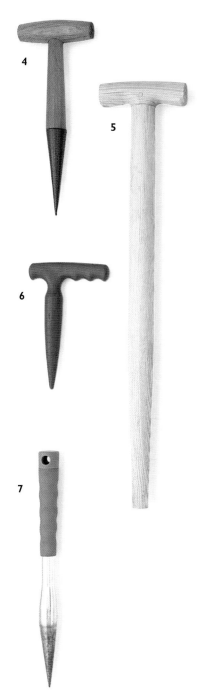

Plant labels

Labelling new plants gives you a written record of their precise names and the date of planting. You can, of course, simply reuse the plastic labels that came with the plants, but starting afresh with durable labels that you have chosen and written on yourself is a much better option. The labels shown here are suitable for outdoor use (for indoor labels, see page 110). All will last for many years, unlike plastic versions, which barely last a year outdoors. The pros and cons of the different materials are described in the relevant captions, which together with their visual appearance will help you select a material. Labels come in many shapes and sizes, and which you choose is mainly down to personal preference. Do you want the labels to be discreet and for your eyes only? Then small metal, wooden or bamboo labels, which you can push down into the ground or use to mark a row of plants, are ideal. If you would prefer highly visible labels, for example to help visitors to your garden identify plants or to display a plant collection, then for larger plants consider oval-shaped labels (often called Victorian or Edwardian tags) as there is plenty of room to write full Latin names. Narrower rectangular labels are available for smaller plants like alpines. Aluminium labels with stems can have the written part of the label bent back for easier reading, while those without stems and with holes punched in them can be hung from trees, shrubs and climbers at eye level.

8 Shown here is a selection of labels made of natural materials. They can be written on with a permanent marker pen. The two bamboo labels on the left are 30cm long and 5cm wide, ideal for marking the position of perennials, bulbs or rows of vegetables. The other labels are made of teak and include types for inserting into the ground, and ones for hanging from stems.

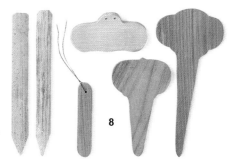

9 Copper is attractive both when new and when it weathers to a verdigris colour. It is rather flimsy compared to aluminium, and labels are best tied on plant stems or wooden stakes rather than pushed directly in the ground. Use a ballpoint pen or a waterproof felt tip to write the plant names.

10 Aluminium is long lasting but flexible, and the colour is discreet. There are two thicknesses: 0.5mm or 0.8mm. A pencil or pen can be used on either, but if you want to use a punching kit to create a permanent label (see below), use the thicker grade.

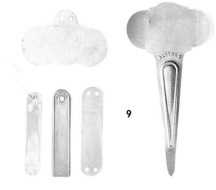

11 Punching kit For a permanent record of trees, shrubs and perennials, the name of the plant can be punched onto 0.8mm thick aluminium. The set of punches shown give a letter height of 5mm. For a professional finish, you can invest in a steel and brass jig that clamps the label and ensures the letters are straight and evenly spaced.

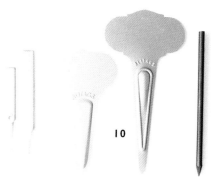

6 L-shaped plastic dibber

This inexpensive, rot-proof plastic dibber is handy for planting very large seeds like pumpkin, sweetcorn or beans, or small bulbs, into well-cultivated soil. Planting depths up to 10cm are marked on the side. The tool has an L-shaped handle and is used like a claw, being quickly prodded into the soil.

7 Straight metal dibber

Metal dibbers make neat holes and are often beautifully shaped to penetrate the soil more easily. This one is made of plated steel and will go down to a depth of 15cm, which is perfect for transplanting small leeks and brassicas. The handle is made of moulded plastic.

Designing with bulbs

Penelope Hobhouse is a garden designer, author and lecturer, who is well known for her imaginative planting in gardens such as Tintinhull in Somerset. Here she shares some of her ideas on using bulbs in borders and explains how she manages to grow a wide range of bulbs in her own Dorset garden, despite having a heavy clay soil.

'I use bulbs in many of my planting schemes, but rather than having a specific place on a planting plan, they are scattered as groups through borders after the main shrubs and perennials are in place. A guiding principle is to match the bulb to the site and soil conditions. In partly shaded positions under deciduous shrubs, small spring bulbs such as chionodoxa, scillas or little anemones like *Anemone nemorosa* or *A. blanda* do well. The bulbs will enjoy a certain amount of shelter, eventually spreading to form a carpet of reliable spring colour and needing little attention.

Alliums are the most important bulbs in my own early summer garden. I add some each year, usually *Allium aflatunense* (now *A. hollandicum*), *A. christophii*, with soft mauve flowers, and the darker *A. hollandicum* 'Purple Sensation' (illustrated on page 39). Of course, tulips are always wonderful. In my relatively modest garden, I grow them mainly in pots, but in my clients' gardens I recommend grouping them in patches of one variety, sometimes anticipating the colour scheme, which evolves during the season. I also like tulips scattered through forget-me-nots or between perennials. Rosemary Verey did this better than anyone else at Barnsley House.

In my own garden, the wet, heavy clay soil makes planting bulbs in autumn back-breaking work, despite the copious amounts of organic matter and gravel that have been added over the years. I find it is far easier to plant dry bulbs in pots during the autumn, overwinter them in a cold frame, and then plant them in the borders in spring. Alliums, camassias, lilies and tulips have all worked well for me in pots.'

Starting bulbs in pots

1 In autumn, plant dry bulbs in pots of compost. Spring-flowering bulbs such as these alliums are hardy, but it is worth putting them in a cold frame over winter to protect them from cold and rain. The cold frame also protects bulbs from larger pests: squirrels love tulips, and mice often nibble crocus bulbs.

2 In spring, the bulbs will sprout and grow, so water the compost if it is dry, and open the lid of the cold frame during mild, dry weather.

3 Plant the young bulbs in groups of three or more where there are gaps in the border. Use a trowel and plant them as you would any other small pot-grown plant. The other advantage of this technique is that, as only growing bulbs are planted out, you are guaranteed to achieve the flowering display you want.

bulb planting

Spring-flowering bulbs can be planted as dry bulbs in the autumn, while summer-flowering bulbs are planted as dry bulbs in the spring. A trowel or a dibber will suffice for planting a few bulbs in a border. To plant in a small area of turf, you could also use a half-moon cutter or a sharp spade to cut and lift a section of turf, plant the bulbs with a spade or trowel, then replace the turf. However, if you want to put in a large number of bulbs or plant extensively in turf, a specialized tool is quicker and ensures the holes are an even depth.

The number of bulbs and how they are spaced out is crucial to the final effect and needs to be decided before choosing a planting tool. Below are two examples of different planting styles, the first requiring a long-handled bulb planter, the second a draw hoe. The use of a short-handled bulb planter is demonstrated on page 40.

Naturalizing bulbs in turf Many spring-flowering bulbs, such as daffodils (*Narcissus*) and the snake's-head fritillary (*Fritillaria meleagris*), can be planted under turf and will push their way up to flower in the grass. Over the years, the bulbs will naturalize to create a carpet of spring colour. You will need an area of grass where the first cut can be delayed until most of the bulb foliage has died back (about six weeks after flowering), such as a gentle slope or a patch of grass near trees or shrubs. Plant the bulbs in early to mid autumn.

1 To plant *Fritillaria meleagris* bulbs in moist, rough turf such as this, first mark out where the cores of turf are to be cut using handfuls of sawdust (the bulbs come packed in sawdust) or similar material.
2 Use a long-handled bulb planter to remove the cores of turf. As the bulbs are small, try not to take out the maximum depth of soil. To remove the core from the planter, either use a broom handle to push it out or make all the holes first so the earth is pushed out of the top of the planter.
3 Place two or three bulbs in the hole and replace the core of turf. If the hole is too deep, break the core in half and add the bottom half in the hole before planting the bulbs, then put in the half with the turf.

Planting in rows Rows of tulips look striking in formal gardens, and planting in rows is an efficient technique when growing tulips or daffodils for cutting. If you have lots of bulbs to plant, the method described here is much quicker than planting each bulb with a planter. Plant daffodils by mid autumn and tulips in late autumn or early winter.
1 Use a garden line to mark out a straight edge. Make a trench at least three times the height of the bulb, using either a draw hoe or a border spade.
2 Space the bulbs evenly along the bottom of the trench, leaving 5–15cm between each bulb.
3 Use a draw hoe or border spade to cover the bulbs with soil. Firm the ground gently with your foot. Label the trench. It is worth protecting tulips against squirrels, who like to dig them up and eat them. A length of chicken wire pegged down over the row is an effective deterrent.

Using planting tools

Planting leeks Use a large or medium-sized dibber to plant leeks in their final positions. This will help them develop a long length of blanched stem. Prior to using the dibber, water the young leek plants, then ease them from the soil with a fork. Separate them out and trim the roots to about 8–10cm; trim any very long leaves, too. Make a long, narrow hole by pressing the dibber into the ground. The deeper the hole, the longer the blanched stem will be, but make sure that some of the leaves are above soil level. Drop a plant into each hole and fill the holes with water to settle the plants in. The leeks will flop at first, but they soon pick up. For medium-sized leeks, make the holes 15cm apart in rows 30cm apart; increase or decrease the spacing to produce bigger or smaller leeks.

Planting tulips Choose a sunny site in the border, the further back the better, so that emerging perennials will hide the dying tulip foliage in early summer. Scatter the bulbs randomly around in patches. Press down on the bulb planter and twist it to make a hole for each bulb. Put one sound bulb in each hole, pointed end uppermost. The planter shown has a lever to release the earth onto the bulb; this works on the well-drained soil favoured by tulips, but soil sticks to the sides of the planter in wet weather. Firm the soil gently with your hands. A typical short-handled bulb planter such as this allows planting up to 15cm deep, which is sufficient for tulips.

Punching labels Punching kits are widely used in botanical gardens, where permanent and clear labels for a large number of plants are essential. The plant names are punched onto aluminium labels so they will never fade. The labels are 0.8mm thick and are clamped in place by the jig. The jig is calibrated so the characters can be evenly spaced and punched in a straight line. Count the letters and spaces in the plant name to work out how much space you will need on the label. Select the letter, place it on the label, then tap it once with the hammer. (One sharp, decisive tap makes a clearer impression than several timid taps.) Make sure you spell the name correctly and hold the letters the right right way up, as mistakes cannot be corrected.

watering and feeding

watering cans and sprayers

All plants need watering, particularly after planting, during dry spells or if they are growing in containers. Watering cans are invaluable for carrying and applying water, and all gardeners need at least one. A watering can is also suitable for mixing and applying liquid feeds and other chemicals; if you want to administer weedkillers with a watering can, it is worth investing in an extra can in a different colour just for this purpose.

The clever part of the watering can is the detachable rose on the end of the spout, which has a series of holes that make the water fall out like rain. Opt for a metal rose as it will be more durable and give a finer spray – if you want the most precision when watering, choose a brass rose that can be fitted so it points upwards. The body and spout of a watering can are either metal or plastic. Cans made of galvanized steel are long lasting, and their appearance improves with age, but they are heavier than plastic ones. Plastic watering cans are lighter, but they weaken with age; the

1 Traditional metal watering can Old cans such as these are often found in shops specializing in by-gones or antique tools. They make attractive and useful watering tools, as long as they do not leak and the rose is in reasonable condition. This can has a short spout with the rose fixed in one position, so is suitable for watering plants growing at ground level.

2 Metal long-reach watering can This classic watering can from Haws has a long spout that makes it invaluable for watering plants at the back of beds or staging. The can is made of zinc-coated steel, and the brass rose can be fitted to point up or down.

3 Plastic long-reach watering can This is a good-quality can made of heavy-duty, injection-moulded plastic, with a brass rose that can be fitted to point up or down. It combines the lightness and quietness of plastic with reasonable durability, and the brass rose allows precision watering.

4 Indoor watering can This elegant can is attractive enough to be left out on display alongside houseplants or in a conservatory. The small capacity (1 litre) makes it easy to lift to water plants displayed high up. The downward curve of the spout ensures the water is applied precisely, either on the compost or into a saucer, but not all over your furnishings.

5 Brass rose Roses are invariably either mislaid or dented before anything happens to the can itself, so it is best to buy a brand of watering can that offers replacement roses. The part where the water comes out of a series of holes – the 'face' – should be made of brass, but the part that attaches to the spout of the can may be metal, with a screw-on thread, or a push-on attachment made of rubber or plastic.

piece of plastic holding the spout to the can or the handle is usually the first part to go. For extra durability it is worth buying a heavy-duty plastic can made by injection moulding.

Outdoor watering cans come in various sizes, from 2.5 litres to 9 litres. Choose a size that you'll be able to carry and use easily when it is full. Remember that it's easier to carry two 4.5- litre cans – one in each hand – than a single 9-litre one. For watering plants in a greenhouse or conservatory, or on windowsills, consider an indoor can, with a smaller capacity (usually 1–2 litres).

Sprayers apply water or other liquids as a fine spray. Most gardeners can get by with an inexpensive hand mister, but the larger sprayers come into their own for tackling problems such as overgrown weedy gardens or for spraying on a large scale, such as in a fruit garden. When you are choosing a sprayer, make sure you pick the right size for the task, bearing in mind how much spraying you are likely to do in one go. Look for sturdy reservoirs that are clearly calibrated and have wide necks for easy filling and cleaning. Spray handles and triggers should be easy to operate, even when you are wearing gloves.

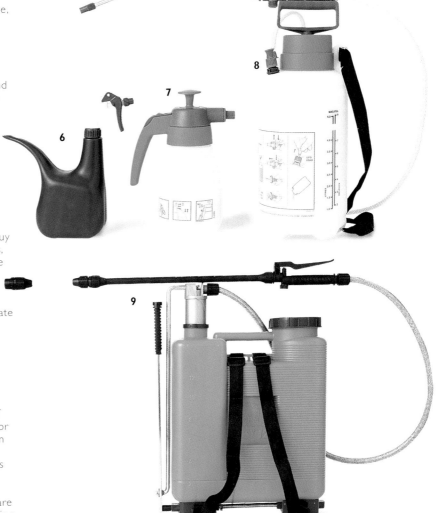

6 Hand mister Plants grown undercover in a heated greenhouse, conservatory or a room within a house often benefit from misting. This increases the humidity, which improves the appearance of the foliage and helps to prevent an infestation of red spider mite. Hand misting is also an excellent way to keep the surface of the compost moist when you are trying to germinate seeds that are sown on the surface. This hand mister also has a pouring spout, so you can either water or mist plants as required in one watering session.

7 Pressure sprayer Owning a pressure sprayer enables you to buy concentrated pesticides, fungicides, weedkillers or fertilizers and dilute them yourself, which is more cost-effective than buying ready-mixed products. This sprayer holds 1.25 litres, an adequate volume of diluted chemicals for dealing with isolated problems. It is available in red or green if you want two sprayers that can be distinguished for different uses.

8 Pressure sprayer with lance A sprayer that can hold 5 litres of diluted chemicals is a useful size for applying weedkiller to a path or an overgrown area of garden, for example. The length of the lance is adjustable, so you can reach into inaccessible places and target weedkillers precisely where they are needed – useful if weeds are coming in under a fence and encroaching on your borders. When the sprayer is not in use, the lance can be clipped into the handle to prevent it getting damaged.

9 Knapsack sprayer Tackling weeds in a large overgrown garden or spraying a sizeable fruit garden can be time-consuming. This piece of equipment will do the job much more quickly than a conventional sprayer. You can make up large quantities of chemicals in one go, and it is easier to carry a load harnessed on your back than one slung over a shoulder. These sprayers are for the serious amateur or professional – be prepared to assemble, clean and maintain them, and to dispose of excess chemicals responsibly. Wear waterproof overalls when spraying, in case the container gets damaged and leaks.

Using a watering can

Used correctly, a simple watering can is a precision watering aid. A good-quality rose will enable you to fine-tune your watering to suit different plants.

I Watering seedlings Attach the rose with the holes pointing uppermost to give the finest spray, so there is no danger of the seedlings being flattened or dislodged. Use tap water for very young plants grown undercover, to reduce the risk of damping-off fungus.

2 Watering young plants Young plants need to be watered regularly during dry spells, as their roots take time to become established. A watering can with the rose fitted downwards will produce rain-like droplets that soak into the surrounding soil without washing it away.

3 Quick watering Some plants need regular and generous watering, for example courgettes and tomatoes as well as shrubs and perennials that are planted in dry summers. It is quicker to use just the spout of the watering can, but if you are in a hurry the force of the water from the spout can wash the soil away and expose the roots of the plant. To avoid this, cut a plastic drinks bottle in half and insert the top half into the ground at the time of planting. This can be filled with water, which will seep slowly into the surrounding soil.

Watering around the garden

Trained as a botanist, Stefan Buczacki writes on all aspects of gardening. Here he gives advice on choosing watering equipment for different parts of the garden and for plants growing under cover, such as tomatoes (see right).

'In the garden, I have found sprinkler hoses are invaluable for establishing long runs of hedging – I secure them in place with metal tent pegs. Seep hoses, which supply water 20–30cm either side of the hose, are useful under cloches as they save having to lift the cloche to water the plants. Over the years I have collected many hose attachments, but it is surprising how few you really need. A gun nozzle that enables you to vary the speed of the water is very useful, as is a stop connector, which allows you to change attachments without getting wet.

Plants in greenhouses need frequent watering, so for tomatoes I use ring culture. This involves digging a trench about 35cm deep and 35cm wide along one side of the greenhouse and lining it with plastic sheeting. This is filled with pea gravel and watered well. I then plant tomato plants in bottomless pots filled with compost and stand the pots on the gravel. Eventually the roots make their way down to take water from the gravel reservoir. This greatly reduces the frequency of watering, from once a day to once a week. In fact, after watering the gravel well beforehand, I have been away for up to a fortnight and returned to find the plants were fine.

In my hothouse, the temperature is 15–18°C all year round, which is ideal for tender ferns, orchids and carnivorous plants. To cut down on watering, I use an automatic misting system controlled by a timer. In the conservatory I grow African violets and species pelargoniums that tolerate the dry environment. These I water by hand using a small watering can.'

hoses, reels and connectors

A hose carries large quantities of water and saves having to struggle to and fro with a watering can. To get the most from a hose, you need an outdoor tap, suitable connectors, and if the hose is to be put away after use, a reel. Fittings such as sprinklers and guns are covered on pages 50–51.

When buying a hose, first work out the length you need to reach the bottom of your garden. Reels of 25–30m are typical, but you can sometimes purchase hose by the metre; buy only the length you require or the nearest length available on a reel, as the longer the hose, the slower the flow rate. If you have a large garden, or if your water pressure is low, it is also important to consider the hose diameter. The larger the diameter, the quicker the water is delivered. A diameter of 13mm is typical; a few 19mm hoses are available.

A hose is made up of several layers (ply), with a smooth inner layer for the water to run through, a reinforcing material such as knitted mesh, then an outer layer, often of PVC, for durability. The thickness and grade of PVC used and the amount of reinforcing material will determine how strong the hose is and how liable it is to kink. If you regularly move a hose around the garden, it is worth buying a 'professional-grade' hose for its extra strength and resistance to kinking. Flat hoses are available, but they have a slower flow rate and are not as durable as round hoses; they also tend to kink.

To prevent your hose ending up in a tangled heap, store it on a reel. A wheeled reel is useful for moving a hose around a large, flat garden; if your outside tap is around a corner or your garden is on a slope, consider a wall-mounted reel.

Once you have set up your hose system, you may want to consider a water timer or water computer. These are fitted between the tap and the hose, and they turn the water on and off at set times, so your garden is watered when you are away or doing something else. Timers are often used in conjunction with other watering systems such as seep hoses, sprinkler hoses or drip irrigation (see page 48). Both examples shown run on a battery (not supplied), which needs to be replaced each year.

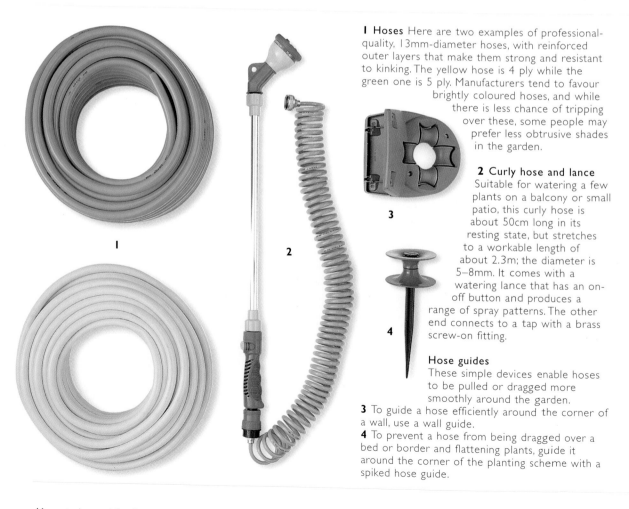

1 Hoses Here are two examples of professional-quality, 13mm-diameter hoses, with reinforced outer layers that make them strong and resistant to kinking. The yellow hose is 4 ply while the green one is 5 ply. Manufacturers tend to favour brightly coloured hoses, and while there is less chance of tripping over these, some people may prefer less obtrusive shades in the garden.

2 Curly hose and lance Suitable for watering a few plants on a balcony or small patio, this curly hose is about 50cm long in its resting state, but stretches to a workable length of about 2.3m; the diameter is 5–8mm. It comes with a watering lance that has an on-off button and produces a range of spray patterns. The other end connects to a tap with a brass screw-on fitting.

Hose guides These simple devices enable hoses to be pulled or dragged more smoothly around the garden.
3 To guide a hose efficiently around the corner of a wall, use a wall guide.
4 To prevent a hose from being dragged over a bed or border and flattening plants, guide it around the corner of the planting scheme with a spiked hose guide.

Hose connectors

These small but invaluable items allow you to take a simple hose and build it into a watering system that is tailor-made to your garden.

5 Traditional connectors are made of brass and are threaded so they screw together; take care not to lose the plastic washers inside.

6 If your outside tap is an old one, safeguard drinking water by fitting a double-check valve or backflow preventer between your hose and the tap. This prevents contaminated water being drawn back up the hose if the mains pressure drops. Modern taps have the valve already fitted, but you can buy one like this to screw into an old tap – you will not then need a tap connector.

7 Plastic connectors are widely used these days; they either screw in or snap-on and are quicker to fit than brass connectors.

8 To join two hoses together, use a repair connector.

9 A stop connector between the end of the hose and a nozzle allows you to disconnect the nozzle without getting drenched or having to go back and turn the tap off.

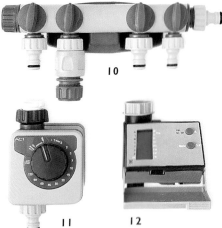

10 4-way connector A handy device that allows you to divide the water supply into four outlets, so you can set up two timed water supplies and still have separate access to water for manual watering.

Water timers

Inserted between the tap and the hose, these devices control whether the water flows down the hose or not, which means they effectively turn water on and off for you. This gives you much more freedom, so you literally don't need to be on tap to have thriving plants.

11 Simple water timer For those who balk at setting the video and like to keep things simple, a timer such as this one is easy to use and can be set to water once a day. These timers work well if you want all the plants to be watered at the same time of day for an equal length of time.

12 Advanced water timer This is a sophisticated system that can be set to water up to three times a day, allowing you to tailor watering to individual plant requirements. It can also be used with a battery-operated rain sensor (not shown), which takes rainfall into account during controlled watering, and with a moisture sensor, which takes into consideration the amount of water in the soil.

13 Portable hose trolley This is a state-of-the-art hose trolley that will roll the hose up for you automatically. It comes complete with hose, nozzle attachments and connectors. One drawback is that you have to assemble the trolley yourself, which can be time-consuming. A variation on this type of trolley has a manual winding system and a telescopic handle that can be adjusted to suit the height of the user and closed down for compact storage.

14 Wall-mounted reel A hose reel that is mounted on a wall is easy to access and saves storage space indoors. The reel shown comes ready-fitted with a hose, and an internal spring allows the user to pull it out to any length up to 20m, and then to walk it back into the reel. A mechanism inside the drum stores the hose neatly and evenly. The wall bracket allows the reel to turn through 180 degrees.

irrigation systems

A system that carries water to plants and applies it gently just where it is needed is a great benefit to gardeners who are short of time, grow lots of plants in containers or live in dry regions. These systems are more efficient than sprinklers because the water is directed to the soil or compost, where it will be most beneficial to the plant. Since it is applied gently, the water has time to soak in rather than run off or evaporate. Use the system in conjunction with a timer or water computer (see page 47) and it will water the garden regularly while you are away or doing something else. The other benefit of using a timer or computer is that there is no danger of forgetting to turn the tap off.

There are various types of irrigation system. Seep hoses work well for plants in the ground that need to be watered for several hours once or twice a week. These hoses can be buried in the soil and left in place for several years. Sprinkler hoses, which are laid on the surface of the soil, are an inexpensive way of keeping rows of plants watered. Drip irrigation systems are useful for container-grown plants on patios, balconies and roof terraces or in greenhouses, which might need watering for 20 minutes or so every day. A gravity-fed watering system uses stored rainwater rather than tap water, so is useful if there are local restrictions on the use of hoses attached to taps.

1 Sprinkler hose This inexpensive tubing is laid out on the surface of the soil and is useful for watering new plantings growing in rows, such as a long run of young hedging plants, fruit or vegetables. This one comprises three channels, each pierced with holes along their length.

2 Seep hose This porous type of hose is also known as a 'soak hose'. It is made of tough rubber derived from recycled tyres, yet is flexible enough to be curved up and down a flower bed. The hose can be buried in the ground, for example to create a bog garden; covered with a mulch and used to water a newly planted border; or left on the soil surface, for example in a vegetable patch.

3 Drip irrigation With this system, small tubes (microtubing) take water from the supply pipe and deliver it to individual containers or plants. The end of the microtubing is fitted with an 'emitter'. There are various types of emitter: some deliver a controlled drip of water, which is ideal for most plants, while others produce a fine spray, which is more suitable for seedlings or for generally increasing humidity in a greenhouse. The system shown here is a simple one for watering hanging baskets. It has small emitters and pegs to secure them in the compost. If the same-sized hanging baskets are used in the same positions each year, it only needs to be set up once.

4 Gravity-fed system Water flows from a water barrel along a supply pipe, then makes its way slowly around circuits of 'gravidrippers' that are pegged to the surface of the soil. Water seeps out of openings into the soil. For the system to work, the barrel, which can be wall-mounted, needs to be positioned higher than the gravidrippers. The manufacturer states that this system will distribute water up to 50 metres away from the barrel.

Setting up a drip irrigation system

Watering systems come ready supplied with pipes and fittings for a small- to medium-sized patio or border or a simple greenhouse. These save you having to work out what connectors you need, but you may have to rearrange your pots or border plantings around the constraints of the pipes and connectors supplied.

For more advanced requirements, for example lots of different-sized containers that are fixed in a particular site, a large vegetable plot or several plant collections with different watering needs, you will need a system that is tailor-made for your garden. Made-to-measure systems are often available from mail-order suppliers. A watering system takes time to plan and set up; it is not something that can be installed quickly just before you go on holiday.

The supply pipe runs from a connector fitted to the tap and should be placed as close to the plants as possible. Microtubing connects the supply pipe to the containers. Lay out all the pipes in their final positions before connecting them. The supply pipe is usually run along the bottom of the house wall and held in place with clips. Where the pipe turns a corner use elbow connectors to avoid kinks.

Another option, instead of microtubing and emitters, is to use a length of sprinkler hose or a leaky hose. This will disperse water along the length of the hose, so it is better for beds and borders than for containers.

1 To fit the microtubing to the master unit, which regulates the pressure, immerse the end in warm water and push it over the end of the master unit.

2 Push an emitter onto the other end of the microtubing. Peg down the emitter to secure it in place (here it is being used to irrigate a container planting).

3 Flush water through the system to remove any dirt, then close off the open pipe, using the end cap supplied, to seal the system. Measure the amount of water collected from each emitter for a given time and compare this to what you would normally provide by hand watering. This will help you decide how long to water and whether any adjustments are needed, for example some plants or container plantings may need more emitters.

Maintaining the system
O Take care not to cut the microtubing when deadheading or harvesting plants.
O The fine holes in the emitters can become blocked. In hard-water areas, limescale residues can be removed with a proprietary limescale remover (such as you might use for a shower head). Fertilizer residues can cause blockages, but flushing the system with warm water will dissolve them.
O Check the microtubing for squirrel damage, which in some areas can be a real problem.
O Drain the pipes at the end of the season.

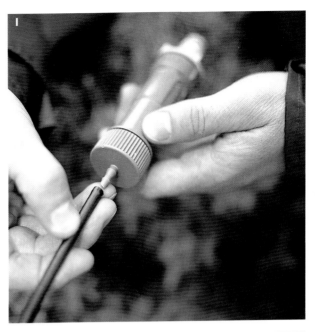

nozzles, guns and sprinklers

The force of water that gushes from the end of a hose is great for quickly filling up watering cans, ponds and children's paddling pools, but not for watering plants, as it washes away soil and compost and the water runs off. Putting your thumb over the end creates a gentler spray, but a nozzle or gun gives much greater control and is more comfortable to use.

To apply light droplets of water over a large area such as a lawn or a newly planted bed, use a sprinkler on the end of a hose. These are popular as little effort is required other then setting them up and turning on the tap, and children love playing in them, but for watering plants they have their drawbacks. To start with, they are not particularly efficient, as water droplets are thrown out and can get carried by the wind, and much of the water applied during the day will simply evaporate. However, they can be useful if you have laid a new lawn or planted a large area, such as under a tree where the soil is dry and the rain does not penetrate. A sprinkler is invaluable for establishing young vegetable plants during a dry spell.

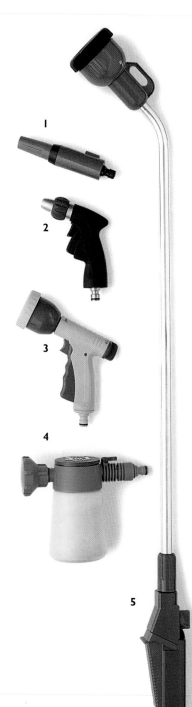

1 Spray nozzle A basic attachment for the end of a hose that allows you to adjust the force of water coming out to deliver anything from a strong jet to a fine mist.

2 Adjustable spray gun An advance on the basic spray nozzle, a spray gun is easier to hold, and you can turn the water flow on and off with the trigger, to avoid wasting water.

3 Rose-head spray gun A versatile spray gun with a rose head that can be set to a light spray for watering seedlings and young plants or a more powerful spray for watering larger plants or cleaning.

4 Feeder This feeder provides a quick and easy way of applying a weekly liquid feed. Simply fit the dispenser, which is ready-filled with concentrated soluble fertilizer, to the end of a hose. When you turn the tap on, water passes through the dispenser and dilutes the fertilizer. Use it with the rose for a gentle spray, remove the rose for faster feeding or buy a separate watering lance for feeding plants in hanging baskets. When the dispenser is empty, you buy a refill. Such feeders are useful if you grow a lot of container plants, but they usually tie you to one brand of fertilizer.

5 Lance The extra reach provided by a lance (80–92cm, depending on the model) makes it invaluable for watering inaccessible plants. This one is a good basic model for gentle watering; other types have adjustable spray patterns for watering either individual plants or groups of plants. There are also multi-purpose lances for watering and cleaning, and ones that are designed to apply water directly to hanging baskets.

6 Rotating sprinkler Designed to sit on the ground, this type of sprinkler has arms that rotate due to the force of the water. Nozzles at the ends of the arms send out water droplets in a circular pattern. The arms and nozzles of this model are made of plastic but brass fittings are also available.

7 Static sprinkler This is a simple, economical sprinkler that delivers droplets of water in a fixed pattern, usually a circle, over a small area. This one is more versatile than many on the market as you can adjust the diameter of the circle and also select one of seven sectors of a circle, for example a semicircle or a quarter circle for watering beds or under trees. A metal spike secures the sprinkler to the ground, so there is no risk of it upending. As the spray on a static sprinkler is fixed, the water has less time to soak into the soil, so keep an eye on the ground while watering and turn the sprinkler off before puddles form.

8 Oscillating sprinkler With an oscillating sprinkler, a metal arm studded with holes moves slowly from side to side to create a rectangular spray pattern. It is ideal for medium-sized gardens with rectangular lawns or beds. The size of the rectangle can be adjusted by setting the arm to do a full swing or a half swing. Check that the arm is actually moving from one side to the other, or only half the area will be watered. If the arm gets bent or damaged, spares can usually be fitted. A more durable model with a brass surround to the holes is available at extra cost.

Watering widsom

O A generous soaking of the soil once a week is more effective than a light sprinkling every day. The aim is to get water down into the root zone, not for it to simply evaporate from the surface. You might need to water two to three times longer than you think from just looking at the surface.

O Reduce evaporation by watering in the evening or early morning; avoid watering at midday. Applying a mulch will help to prevent evaporation.

O Water is a valuable resource, so conserve as much as you can by saving rainwater and by reusing water from the house. Water used for washing vegetables or hand-washing crockery can be applied to soil around plants, but do not use very greasy water or water containing strong chemicals.

9 Pulse-jet sprinkler This powerful sprinkler can cover a circular area up to about 26m in diameter, depending on the hose diameter and the water pressure. A single jet rotates in a series of pulses, which gives the water a chance to soak into the ground before the next pulse. It can also be set to cover a section of a circle.

10 Mobile sprinkler Also known as 'travelling sprinklers' or 'water tractors', mobile sprinklers come into their own for watering large lawns because they avoid the need to keep moving the sprinkler (and hose) around the lawn by hand. This one is called the 'Rain Train', and it works by moving around the lawn along the route of a hose laid on the ground; it is useful on an L-shaped lawn, for example. While on its journey, the arms revolve and let out water droplets.

11 Ornamental sprinkler Who says sprinklers have to be purely functional? This sculptural copper sprinkler is called 'Orchid no. 2' and is one of several 'WaterDance' designs created by Cyr Smith of Smith & York in the USA. They are now also made and sold in other countries, under licence. The stem is inserted into the ground by prongs at the bottom, and the head sits on the stem. When the water is turned on the head rotates and creates a wonderful display. If you have high water pressure, you will need to turn the tap on slowly; otherwise, the head will shoot off. Like all copperwork, this sprinkler can be left out all year, and it will eventually take on a verdigris patina.

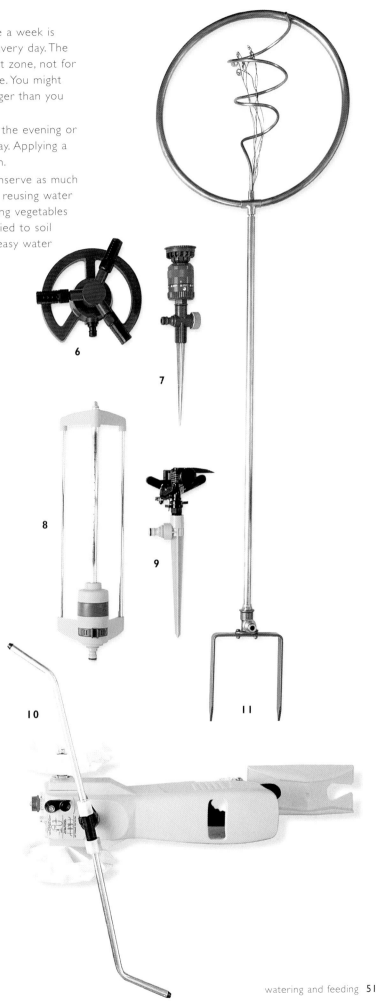

6

7

8

9

10

11

water storage

Stored water is a valuable reserve if hosepipe bans are in force or your water is metered or you do not have an outside tap. A water barrel will collect and store rainwater from the gutters and downpipe of a house or outbuilding. Rainwater is free from lime, so in a hard-water area, it is best to use such water for acid-loving plants growing in containers.

Water barrels were originally made of wood, but these days plastic is widely used. A barrel is not the most space-efficient shape to put against a wall, and there are now box-shaped containers that save space in smaller gardens. Before choosing a water barrel, decide on a location and consider how the surrounding space will be used – is it in the middle of an access route, for example? If so, perhaps a wall-mounted unit might help. If you want to install a large barrel, a rain diverter and a long hose give you the option of positioning it away from the downpipe. Alternatively, consider having several small barrels placed around the garden rather than one very large one.

Choose a barrel with a lid to stop insects and debris getting into it and contaminating the water, and as a precaution against children climbing in. Make sure it is high enough to get a watering can under the tap easily – you can either buy a stand, choose a barrel with legs or make a platform of bricks.

A rain diverter and a hose are useful for moving stored water around the garden. Capillary matting, which is usually used in greenhouses and conservatories, is another way of moving water from a reservoir. There are also irrigation kits that are designed to work from a water barrel rather than a tap (see page 48).

1 Round water barrel A typical plastic barrel with several good features such as the screw-in tap and childproof lid. This is one of the smaller barrels with a height of 80cm, a diameter of 23cm and a capacity of 168 litres. Larger sizes are available.

2 Stand This purpose-built stand raises a water barrel 38cm off the ground, making it is easy to place a watering can under the tap. The stand is 71cm in diameter.

3 Wall-mounted water butt This slim-line butt is mounted on a wall between a downpipe and drain. It will fit a standard square or round pipe and has a rain diverter built in, so once it is full, any excess rain will go down the drain. It holds 100 litres, but takes up very little ground space, being 1.2m high, 45cm wide and only 23cm deep. Note that the tap is inserted on the side, leaving clear access past the butt.

4 Rain diverter A simple device that can be inserted into a round or square domestic downpipe to divert water elsewhere. For example, a diverter can be fitted between a downpipe and water barrel to automatically stop the barrel overflowing after heavy rain. Connecting a long hose (not supplied) between the rain diverter and a water barrel gives you the freedom to position the barrel in a completely different location, perhaps in a greenhouse where the water would then be warmed to room temperature.

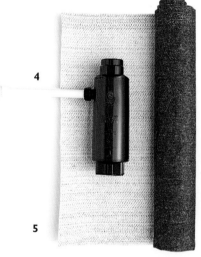

5 Capillary matting This 3mm-thick cotton and polyester material holds lots of water and is used to water small pots from underneath. Lay it on a flat, level surface, water it well and place the pots on it. The dark side of the matting hides algae and compost spills, so this side is usually used uppermost; the reflective white side is useful where light levels are low.

recycling

Nature will eventually recycle plant waste, but the process can be speeded up by techniques such as composting. Traditionally, this meant building a large timber bin at the bottom of the garden and filling it with garden waste. Today there is an environmental need for more people to recycle not only garden waste but kitchen waste, and several products have been devised to encourage recycling.

Ready-made compost bins and kits are now widely available, and there are a few attractive or discreet ones worth seeking out. The larger the bin, the easier it is to generate and retain the warmth needed for the bacteria to break down plant waste. Small bins need more maintenance; for example, they need to be insulated in cold weather. Leaves can be collected in any size of container with no insulation as they are broken down by fungi to make leafmould. If your garden does not produce enough garden waste for a compost bin, you could recycle kitchen waste in a wormery.

Pruning shrubs and trees and trimming hedges generates large amounts of woody waste, which takes far longer to compost down than green waste. Shredding the prunings reduces their bulk, and they will rot down much quicker. If you only need to deal with prunings once a year, it's best to hire a shredder, but if your garden produces lots of woody waste through the year, it's worth buying one.

1 Plastic compost bin This kit allows you to quickly and easily make a small compost bin or leafmould enclosure to a size of your choice. Simply open out the stiff plastic mesh to the diameter required and hold it in place with the clips provided. Another advantage of this bin is that it is easy to dismantle and store. However, it is flimsier than a wooden bin, so to keep it upright either wedge it in somewhere, such as between a fence and a shed, or bury the bottom in the ground.

2 Wormery At its simplest, a wormery is a dustbin that has been modified to house brandling worms, which will break down kitchen waste into compost. The compost is harvested when the bin is full. This composter goes one stage further, as it has four storeys that can be harvested little and often.

3 Sieve Before using garden compost or leafmould to make your own potting compost, sieve it to remove any lumps of partially composted material (these can be returned to the bin for further composting).

4 Wooden compost bin Designed to look like a beehive, this bin deserves to be put on full view rather than hidden at the bottom of the garden. The waste is added through the hinged lid, and the compost is taken out through the removable bottom panel. Made of pressure-treated pine, the bin is 95cm high and 65 x 65cm wide and deep.

5 Shredder Always make a point of seeing and hearing different shredders in action before you buy one, as some clog up easily and are a fiddle to unblock, and some are incredibly noisy. It is well worth paying extra for a quieter shredder, although they often take a bit longer to shred. To avoid having to stop and clear blockages, get a machine that can cope with thicker branches and is easy to clear. This is one of the quieter shredders, and it cuts branches up to 3.5cm in diameter, using a toothed drum rather than a blade. It has a mechanism for clearing blockages easily without dismantling the hopper. A black sack for collecting the shreddings is provided.

Quick compost

If space is limited, you could buy a roll-up plastic bin and fill it with garden waste all in one go, during an autumn clear-up, for example. The compost will be ready in three to four months, when the bin can be dismantled.

I Site the bin on bare ground in a location that is out of view but easily accessible. Collect together green garden waste. Mix all the ingredients together and pile them into the bin. Water the contents if they are dry and cover them with old carpet and a sheet of plastic or bubble insulation. The aim is to keep the contents warm and moist, but not sodden. To speed up the process, turn out and mix the contents a couple of times.

2 The compost is ready when it is impossible to identify the original ingredients. You can then dismantle the bin to leave a pile of garden compost. Use this to enrich the soil before planting or as a mulch on borders or around vegetables, or mix it with topsoil or potting compost and use it to fill raised beds or large tubs. If you will not be using the compost immediately, store it in strong plastic bags or cover it with a sheet of polythene and secure the edges.

Setting up a wormery

A wormery turns kitchen waste into organic material for the garden, but it cannot be used for garden waste. Site it near the house for easy access. This one has a series of trays that are added as the worm population increases.

I To set up the first tray, lay down a sheet of the cardboard, then the bedding, then spread the worms on top. Cover them with the coir mat and put on the lid. Once the worms have filled the first tray, remove the mat and add the next tray. During cold spells, the wormery should be insulated with bubble insulation. Heavy rain can flood the wormery, so place it in a sheltered location.

2 When adding extra trays, remove the mat and make sure the bottom of the new tray touches the bedding material underneath – these two steps will allow the worms to move up. Add kitchen waste such as fruit and vegetable peelings, and tea bags, then replace the mat. No more than a 2cm layer of kitchen waste should be added over half the surface area of the tray at any one time.

pruning
and cutting

pruning tools

Secateurs or hand pruners are essential for general pruning and for cutting down perennials. They are also useful for taking woody cuttings, harvesting cut flowers and deadheading. As they are in almost constant use throughout the year, every gardener needs his or her own pair.

These precision tools will cut through stems around 12–15mm in diameter (half this if cutting through dead wood), without damaging either the secateurs or the plant. For tackling stems between 15mm and 3cm in diameter, you'll need a pair of basic long-handled loppers or a pole pruner. Loppers are not essential for every garden, but come into their own for renovating more mature shrubs. Pole pruners are designed to work above head height and can tackle branches up to 3cm in diameter. For even thicker branches, you'll need a saw (see page 60).

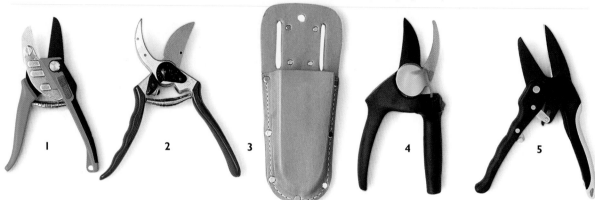

1   2   3   4   5

1 Anvil secateurs An anvil action is ideal for dealing with dead wood, which tends to be harder to cut. These secateurs have a coated blade, well-shaped handles and a safety catch that is easy to use. This version is made for right-handers only, but left-handed models are available.

2 Bypass hand secateurs Bypass secateurs are preferred for making precise pruning cuts. Shown here are Felco no. 2, favoured by many professionals. Felco secateurs are gardening classics and come with a lifetime guarantee. They are made of forged metal alloy with rubber-coated handles. The carbon-steel blades stay sharp for a long time and are easy to sharpen and replace. There is a wide range of other models, including versions for small hands, large hands and several left-handed designs.

3 Holster Keeping your secateurs in a holster while you are working means you will have less chance of losing or damaging them, and they will always be to hand when you need them.

6

4 Gear secateurs A gear-action mechanism and rolling handles enable these bypass secateurs to cut very efficiently. The carbon-steel blades are sharp, but are easier to replace than sharpen, because of a non-stick coating. They are suitable for right-handers only.

5 Ratchet secateurs A lightweight tool with a ratchet action makes pruning easier for anyone with a weak grip. These tools are inexpensive, yet the non-stick, carbon-steel blades are sharp and the handles comfortable. Ratchet secateurs tend to be replaced rather than repaired, but heavier-duty versions may have the option of fitting new blades.

6 Comfort-fit secateurs These two pairs of secateurs are part of a range that offers small, medium and large versions to suit different hand sizes. Shown here are the bypass ones for small and large hands; the same sizes are available with anvil heads, too. These models have a non-slip grip, angled cutting heads to reduce wrist strain and buffers to reduce jarring. The blades have a non-stick coating and are replaceable.

Cutting action Secateurs and loppers use one or more of the following actions:

O **Bypass action** Bypass secateurs have a cutting blade and a non-cutting blade to hold the stem: the blades move past each other to make a slicing cut.

O **Anvil action** Tools with an anvil action have only one moving blade – the cutting blade – which comes down onto a stationary anvil, making a neater chop than a slicing action.

O **Ratchet-anvil** A mechanism similar to the anvil action, but the moving blade is attached to a ratchet and the cut is made as a series of small bites. The mechanism can tackle thicker stems, but it takes longer to cut.

O **Gear action** A recent innovation that makes the cutting action more efficient. A gear mechanism is used instead of a lever between the handle and head.

Choosing pruning tools The better-quality secateurs are usually made of two solid forged pieces of steel bolted together. The handles are coated in PVC or rubber for comfort, and the blades are either carbon steel or stainless steel. They are attached separately, making them easy to sharpen and replace. Such tools should last a lifetime: the handles will not break and blades and other parts such as springs are easy to maintain and replace. Professional gardeners and serious amateurs tend to choose top-quality secateurs, but inexpensive tools with plastic handles and non-replaceable blades, often with a non-stick coating, are adequate if you do not have lots of shrubs to prune. They are lightweight, so less tiring to hold for long periods, and the handles may be moulded for comfort. If a blade cannot be replaced, the useful life of the whole tool depends entirely on whether it can be sharpened; those with a coating cannot.

With secateurs, assess how comfortable the handles feel in your hand. In some designs the handles are not long enough for people with large hands; if you have small hands, check that the secateurs sit well in your palm when they are fully open, and are not too heavy. The safety catch that holds the blades closed should be easy to operate with one hand. If you have a weak grip, try a ratchet design. It is possible to order left-handed anvil and bypass secateurs. With loppers and pole pruners, check the weight and balance. Work out how far the handle of a pole pruner extends. When comparing brands, look at the different ways of activating the cutting blade; most work by a cord or lever. Find out what accessories are available – a sawing attachment is essential for tackling larger branches.

7 Bypass loppers Traditional loppers are heavy-duty tools, and most people find them tiring to use for long periods, particularly when working above chest height. The type shown are inexpensive, cut efficiently and are not too heavy. Although the coated, non-stick blades are not replaceable, this pair is ideal for occasional use. Loppers with shorter handles are lighter, but you lose the extra leverage and reach. If these are important to you, one of the newer gear- or ratchet-action loppers may be the answer.

8 Gear-action loppers This is one of a new series of loppers designed with a gear action for more efficient cutting. Aluminium handles also reduce their weight. The coated, non-stick blades are sharp and should wear well, but they cannot be replaced. There are different sizes for tackling branches within the 2.5–4.5cm range; most models have a bypass action, but one large anvil type is available.

9 Ratchet loppers The ratchet action allows wood to be cut in easy steps, so branches thicker than normal can be tackled (4–5.5cm diameter is claimed, depending on the model). The handles are made of lightweight polyamide, and the carbon-steel blades are replaceable.

10 Pole pruner A safer alternative to pruning from a ladder: the cutting blades are at the end of a long pole, enabling you to reach overhanging branches while standing on the ground. Pole pruners are also ideal for reaching into the centre of mature prickly shrubs. They are lightweight and easy to use, even for those of a small build. Newer versions have telescopic handles. This version has stainless-steel blades with a non-stick coating.

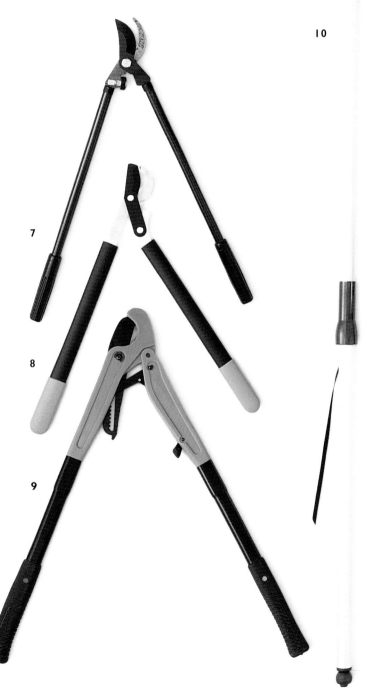

10

7

8

9

Using pruning tools

1 Pruning twiggy shrubs Small, twiggy shrubs such as blue spiraea (*Caryopteris*) and lavender (*Lavandula*) are best cut back annually, as long as you start when the plants are young. In spring, once the frosts are over and new growth appears at the base, use secateurs to cut back nearly all the previous year's growth. Excellent foliage and flowers will be produced on the new growth.

2 Renovating mature shrubs This involves cutting some of the older, thicker stems right back with a heavy-duty tool. Loppers allow you to cut medium-sized branches of thorny or spiny shrubs, such as this pyracantha, at arm's length. To use these ratchet loppers, one handle (with the red spot) is held still and the other handle (with a green spot) is moved to make the cut.

3 Pruning mature trees Use a pole pruner to cut the thinner dead wood from the high branches of mature trees, such as this weeping willow (*Salix*). This prevents the tree becoming congested, improves its appearance, and allows more light through to the ground.

Pruning English Roses

David Austin has an international reputation as a rose breeder and author. Together with his son, David Austin Junior, he runs the highly successful David Austin Roses near Wolverhampton, comprising a nursery, plant centre, design service and a rose garden containing over 700 varieties. David Austin is best known for his English Roses, which are bred to combine the charm and fragrance of old roses with the colour range and long flowering period of modern roses. Their shrubby growth makes them ideal for mixed borders, and they are effective as climbers. Here David gives some tips on growing and pruning English Roses.

'To get the most impact from English Roses, I plant them in groups of three or more of one variety, spaced about 50cm apart so they grow together to form 'one' impressive shrub (see opposite for an example using 'Sophy's Rose'). When it comes to pruning English Roses, I would like to stress that it is very easy. They need no pruning immediately after planting, and in subsequent years they should simply be reduced by between one- and two-thirds in mid to late winter. Choose a sunny day when the ground is not too muddy. While it is important to remove any dead or diseased stems, it is not necessary to remove all the weaker growth, as both the weak and the strong growth draw up nutrients at the start of the growing season and help to produce a stronger plant. As for the pruning cuts, they should ideally be made just above a bud, but don't worry about the exact position. To prune my roses, I use Felco no. 2 secateurs.'

saws

Saws can tackle stems and branches that are too thick for secateurs and loppers. A basic pruning saw will deal with branches from 2.5 to 10cm in diameter, making it an essential tool for a garden with trees and large shrubs. Pruning saws usually cut on the pull stroke only and are easy to use in a confined space.

For removing thicker branches or cutting up logs, bow saws tend to be quicker. They have a thinner blade to reduce friction and cut on the push as well as the pull stroke, making light work of branches and logs up to 25cm in diameter. The blade must be kept taut and secured between the two arms of the tubular steel bow. Anyone renovating a mature or neglected garden full of hedges, shrubs and trees should invest in both tools.

Choosing saws Hold a saw like a pistol to see if the handle is comfortable, and check the ease of use and quality of any folding mechanisms, locks or tightening knobs. It is worth paying extra for a pruning saw with ground teeth. These cut very quickly compared to cheap versions with teeth pressed from sheet metal. Look for a saw with a blade that resists rust – one that is chrome-plated, for example – or that can be easily replaced. Blade lengths vary: as a guide, the blade needs to be at least twice as long as the wood is thick.

1 Folding pruning saw A blade that folds away into the handle is a sensible safety feature on a pruning saw. In this model, a red button operates a lock that holds the blade open or closed. The 18cm blade is chrome-plated steel alloy with ground teeth, while the handle grip is formed from ribbed polypropylene, with a hole for hanging it up.

2 Pruning saw This is a slightly heavier-duty pruning saw with a 25cm blade of chrome-plated carbon steel with ground teeth, capable of cutting branches up to 13cm in diameter. The beech-wood handle is shaped for comfort and can be hooked over a branch. A pruning saw can also be used for cutting through tree or shrub roots, dividing fibrous-rooted perennials or cutting turf.

3 Scabbard Use a scabbard to protect the blade of non-folding pruning saws from damage and to reduce the risk of accidents. This version is made of wood and has a belt attachment.

4 Bow saw This bow saw has a handle that protects the knuckles while sawing and a pointed nose to give better access in awkward spaces. The 53cm steel blade is hardened and tempered, while the peg-tooth edge means it can be used to cut both green and dry wood. The knob at the end of the handle increases the tension on the blade and releases it for replacement. A blade protector that snaps into place is supplied.

5 Rootcutter The straight, stiff, 15cm blade makes easy work of dividing tough perennials or trimming shrub roots before repotting. The tempered carbon-steel blade is fixed into the plastic handle, so is not replaceable. Use the loop attached to the handle to hang it in a safe place after use.

6 Saw attachment Although it is a bit fiddly to fit, this is a worthwhile accessory for a pole pruner (see page 57), enabling the tool to tackle thicker branches.

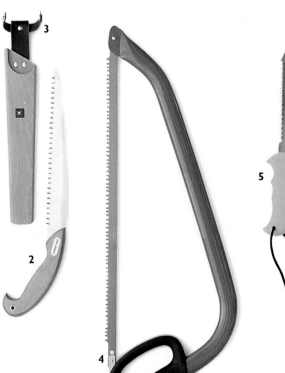

Using saws

Pruning saw An elder (*Sambucus nigra*) with thick vertical stems growing up from the base is a typical example of the tight corner a gardener is faced with when renovating or controlling a mature shrub. A pruning saw is small enough to be used in the narrow gap formed by angle of the branch and the stem. Leaning into the shrub and holding the blade as far down the stem as possible, saw the branch. As it cuts on the pull stroke only, a pruning saw takes a while to cut through a branch.

Bow saw Use a bow saw where there is plenty of room to move the whole saw freely backwards and forwards, for example when cutting horizontal branches from a mature tree, felling a small tree or sawing logs. As it cuts on both the push and pull strokes, it is quicker to use than a pruning saw. Here a bow saw is used to cut a horizontal side branch off a weeping willow tree. The branch is taken off in stages to stop the bark tearing under the weight of the branch. The first cut is made about 30–45cm from the trunk, sawing about halfway through the branch from below. The second cut is made from above, just a few centimetres further from the trunk than the undercut. Saw until the end of the branch falls off. Make another undercut, then make the final cut directly above (see right) to remove the rest of the branch. Note the swelling where the branch joins the main trunk; this 'collar' should be left intact. Never saw above head height; use a ladder to reach high branches and get someone to steady it for you.

Rootcutter Use a rootcutter when pruning roots growing in soil or compost. This will save wear and tear on more expensive pruning saws and prevent them from becoming soiled, which can spread plant diseases. To root-prune a tree or shrub that has been growing in a wooden barrel for many years, such as this Japanese maple (*Acer palmatum* 'Sango-kaku'), expose the rootball and root-prune the edges to reduce its size. Cut away the old, damaged or encircling roots but leave as many of the small fibrous roots as possible. Once the rootball has been reduced, put the plant back in its pot and fill the gaps between the rootball and the sides of the container with fresh compost. If this is done towards the end of the dormant season, the tree will put on attractive young growth in spring and summer.

trimming tools

These tools are primarily for trimming hedges or topiary, although they are often used for other trimming tasks like edging lawns or cutting back small shrubs, climbers or perennials with lots of thin stems. Hedge shears, also known as garden shears, are the basic hand tools for cutting a hedge. They consist of two cutting blades joined in the middle, a knob to adjust the tension of the blades, and two handles. The handles are usually made of wood, tubular steel or moulded nylon. Handle length and orientation varies, as does the shape; some have rubber grips or buffers.

A powered hedgetrimmer will trim a hedge much quicker than hedge shears: if you have a long hedge, this might mean a chore that used to take all morning or afternoon could be completed in an hour. Typically, powered tools can cut twiggy growth up to either 11mm or 15mm in diameter. Electric hedgetrimmers are light, easy to use and give the neatest finish. For hedges that are too far away from an electricity supply, the powered options are either a petrol or a rechargeable hedgetrimmer. Petrol trimmers (not shown) are powerful tools, more suited to the professional gardener who is used to the weight, noise and vibration. Rechargeable trimmers are quiet and there is no cable to worry about. However, they are suitable for cutting only a short run of hedge, as they are slower than electric ones.

A number of tools can be used for making topiary. A powered hedgetrimmer may be suitable for large topiary on top of a hedge, but hedge shears, trimming shears or topiary shears are preferable for small- to medium-sized pieces as they offer closer cutting control. Trimming or topiary shears, which are used one-handed, give a particularly crisp outline to smaller pieces, and many topiary enthusiasts swear by them.

Choosing trimming tools

It is essential to try hedge shears in the shop. Hold them at chest height, and open and close them vigorously several times. The action should feel smooth with no jarring to your wrists as the blades close. The shears should have the right weight and balance for you – too heavy and trimming will be tiring, but be wary of just opting for the smallest shears, as these will take longer to cut the hedge. Shears with an overall length of about 45cm and a cutting length of about 20cm will suit most people.

Look for durable shears with handles that are securely attached to the blades, and a central knob that is strong and easy to use. Blades should stay sharp and be resistant to rust. Most are carbon steel and either have a non-stick coating or are hardened and tempered. Straight-edged blades with no coating are easier to resharpen than wavy-edged ones. Shears with telescopic handles are useful for high hedges or to save you bending, but check the handles are well made and will not work loose.

Trimming shears come with different blade lengths. For detailed topiary, 9cm blades will give the most precise cut; they are also light enough for those with small hands to use for other purposes. Check the squeezing action is comfortable for you. Blades lengths of 13–15cm will cope with larger-scale trimming tasks more quickly (see pages 116–117). To protect the shears and to ensure you have them readily to hand, it is advisable to keep them in a leather holster.

When choosing a powered tool, once you have decided on the power source. try the handles on different brands to see which are most comfortable and easy to use (most have two-handed control, which is a useful safety feature). Blade lengths vary. Around 40cm gives a good compromise between speed of cutting and the problems of extra weight and harder control that come with very long blades.

1 Notched shears A durable pair of shears with chrome-steel blades and nylon handles. The cutting notch near the pivot is for tackling thicker stems. The handles are shaped like a wishbone and have a buffer to reduce jarring.

2 Gear-action shears A gear mechanism reduces the effort needed for cutting. The blades have a non-stick coating and a wavy edge, so cannot be resharpened easily. The wooden handles have a rubber buffer to reduce jarring.

3 Telescopic shears The tubular steel handles of these shears extend from 33cm to 52cm, and can be locked in position to prevent slipping. The blades have a non-stick coating.

4 Trimming shears Originally developed from sheep shears, these one-handed shears are invaluable for precise cutting over a small area. They are made of hand-forged carbon steel and have a spring action. The hardened and tempered blades are easy to resharpen, but must be well cared for to prevent rusting. They can be used for topiary, deadheading herbaceous plants, harvesting herbs, clipping conifers and cutting back aquatic plants.

5 Topiary shears These have evolved from trimming shears and are made of the same materials, but they are intended specifically for topiary work. They are designed to give greater cutting control; the handle is easier to squeeze.

6 Swivel shears The blades of these one-handed shears can be adjusted to swivel through 180 degrees. Use them to trim new growth on topiary and small, twiggy shrubs. They are also useful for trimming short runs of lawn edging. There is an easy-to-use safety catch, and the blades are made of polished steel. These shears are suitable for left- or right-handers.

7 Electric hedgetrimmer An electric tool cuts a hedge quickly and neatly. As long as you take sensible precautions with the cable, it is easy to use. The cable should be put over your shoulder when the tool is in use and checked regularly for wear and tear. As with all electric tools, the circuit should be protected by an RCD (residual current device) to prevent an electric shock from a cut cable. This model has a 37cm blade; longer versions are available.

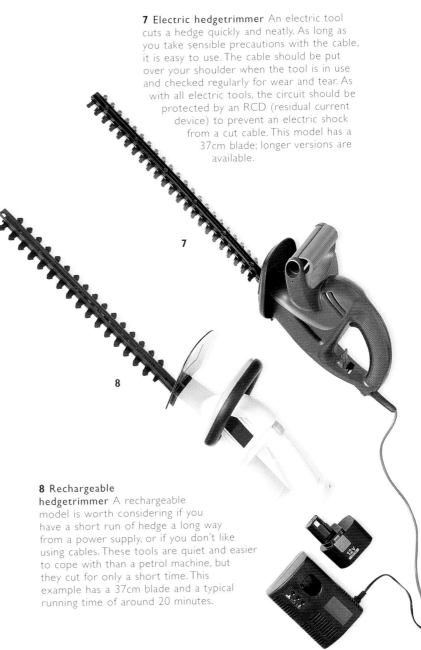

8 Rechargeable hedgetrimmer A rechargeable model is worth considering if you have a short run of hedge a long way from a power supply, or if you don't like using cables. These tools are quiet and easier to cope with than a petrol machine, but they cut for only a short time. This example has a 37cm blade and a typical running time of around 20 minutes.

Using trimming tools

Regular trimming of shoots stimulates the production of lots of side shoots and so gives plants such as hedging and some shrubs a compact growth habit. A dense hedge makes a better boundary or divider than an open, leggy one. Many shrubs look neater or can be kept within bounds by trimming, although this is largely down to personal preference rather than necessity. Trimming tools such as garden shears or hedgetrimmers are quicker than secateurs at taking off lots of thin, twiggy shoots, although secateurs are often used for training young plants into hedges. When trimming a hedge, a length of string stretched between canes at either end of the hedge will provide you with a guide for making a straight, level cut at the required height.

1 Hedge shears Despite the increasing popularity of power tools, hand tools such as these hedge shears will produce the neatest, crispest finish; it is also worth using hand tools when establishing the framework of a hedge as they give you more control. Use shears that have been well serviced, that is with clean, sharp blades and moving parts that have been oiled. Hold the shears so the blades are parallel to the line of the hedge. Here a three-year-old yew hedge is being trained by having its lateral shoots cut back by a third to half their length.

2 Hedgetrimmer Wear goggles to protect your eyes from prunings. If you are using an electric tool connected to the mains, only trim in dry weather and make sure there is protection from an RCD (residual current device), so that if the cable is accidentally cut, the power will be stopped automatically. Trail the cable over your shoulder so it is out of the way of the blade.
 Choose a hedgetrimmer that you can hold and control easily rather than one with the longest blade. Hold it with both hands and keep the blade parallel to the sides or top of the hedge while using a sweeping action. Do not hold the hedgetrimmer above shoulder height as you will have less control – if you need to tackle a tall hedge, use a free-standing ladder or a hedge-cutting platform.

Creative hedging

Dutch designer and plantsman Piet Oudolf uses plant forms and colours as well as less tangible qualities such as light and movement to create gardens of great drama and atmosphere. He has designed gardens and parks throughout Europe, and his own garden and nursery near Hummelo in the Netherlands (see opposite) is a place of pilgrimage for his many admirers. Although Piet is best known for his naturalistic perennial planting, many of his gardens contain interesting hedges. Here he urges us to be more imaginative with our own hedges.

'Many people consider hedges just in terms of boundaries around a garden, but we should think of them as wonderful images that can be clipped into beautiful shapes. At the rear of my own garden, I have used clipped yew to create living screens that make a formal contrast to the preceding perennials. I also have a mixed hedge of beech (*Fagus sylvatica*) and hornbeam (*Carpinus betulus*), cut into informal cloud shapes. Many other deciduous plants can be woven into informal hedges, including dogwood (*Cornus mas*), field maple (*Acer campestre*), chaenomeles and amelanchier. When planning hedges in your own garden, make a scale drawing to get the position right. Hedges should be considered and planted first as they are permanent elements that provide structure.
 When a hedge is young, I shape it by hand with garden shears. Once the form is there and it has a tight growth habit, I switch to an electric hedgetrimmer. Whatever you use, the important thing is to have a sharp blade and to clip at the right angle. I cut the yew in June, with sometimes a second cut in September. The cloud hedges are pruned with an electric hedgetrimmer in winter.'

knives and scissors

A penknife or secateurs will suffice for many cutting tasks, but if you have a particular interest such as propagation or flower arranging, or if you grow fruit and vegetables, there are specialized knives and scissors that are worth considering.

A small, sharp, clean blade is vital for taking cuttings and for smoothing rough pruning cuts. It is best to keep these tools for their particular uses rather than employ them for rougher tasks like cutting string or harvesting vegetables. For the latter, you could use a penknife or harvest knife. Asparagus can be harvested with a special knife that is shaped to cut the spears underground. Knives are usually made of high-quality carbon steel or stainless steel, and most can be resharpened.

The scissors and flower shears featured here are designed for lighter, more delicate work than the secateurs on page 56.

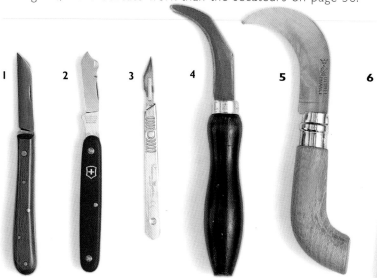

1   2   3   4   5   6   7

1 Grafting knife With a thinner blade than a penknife, and a straight edge, this knife is designed for making the straight cuts needed for grafting. It is also the best choice for a general-purpose knife and can be used for taking and trimming cuttings, and light pruning tasks such as removing side shoots. This example is one of the Tina knives, which are favoured by professionals as the blades keep their cutting edge well.

2 Budding knife A specialized knife, with a projection on the blade called a 'bark lifter', which is used for opening a cut so that budding material can be inserted. It is worth buying if you want to propagate roses, fruit and other shrubs by budding. This one is made by Victorinox, who also make the original Swiss Army knife. It has a stainless-steel blade that holds its sharpness well and folds away into a nylon handle.

3 Scalpel A scalpel with disposable blades is sharp and thin enough to cut soft plant tissue, for example when taking leaf cuttings. It is widely used in plant tissue culture as the whole tool can be sterilized by dipping it in white spirit and holding it over a flame. It is also useful for amateur gardeners who want to propagate herbaceous plants or houseplants.

4 Harvest knife A good all-purpose harvesting knife with a curved blade of carbon steel that can be resharpened. It is worth buying if you grow a lot of vegetables as it will speed up harvesting and save spoiling propagation or pruning knives. Use it for cutting heads of cauliflowers, cabbage and hearted lettuce, and for trimming root crops such as parsnips and carrots. This knife does not fold away, so store it carefully (a leather sheath was provided with this brand).

5 Pruning knife A strong knife with a curved blade that folds into a wooden handle. Designed for pruning young trees, it is also called a 'peach pruner'. This one has carbon-steel blades and wooden handles, which are joined by a metal ring that is twisted to lock the blade in position.

6 Asparagus knife The priority for most knives is to be sharp, but the asparagus knife is an exception. This tool needs to be strong enough to thrust into the soil with a jabbing action to harvest the asparagus spears underground. This one is a top-of-the-range handcrafted tool with a turned yew handle and a serrated blade.

The blades are often narrower, so can be used with minimum risk to the surrounding plants. A cut-and-hold device minimizes handling of the stems and so improves the keeping quality of cut flowers; it also makes it less likely that you will drop deadheaded flowers.

It is important to hold knives, scissors and shears before buying, particularly if your hands are larger or smaller than average. If a knife blade folds into the handle for safety, check it is not too stiff or loose, and check any locking mechanism. Knives with one flat edge, scissors and shears are generally designed for right-handers, but left-handed versions of some tools are available. All cutting edges should be cleaned after use and wiped dry before they are folded up or stored (see page 8).

Successful cutting and harvesting

O Pick leafy salads in the cool of a summer evening or in the early morning – plant cells are more turgid then, so the salads will be crisper.

O To prolong flowering displays, particularly of container-grown plants, cut off the flowers as soon as they start to fade, then water and feed the plant. This will encourage more flowers to form.

O When harvesting flowers for drying, such as helichrysum, choose a warm, dry day and cut the flowers just before they open (they often continue to open while drying).

O To ensure top-quality cut flowers and fruit, handle them as little as possible after harvesting.

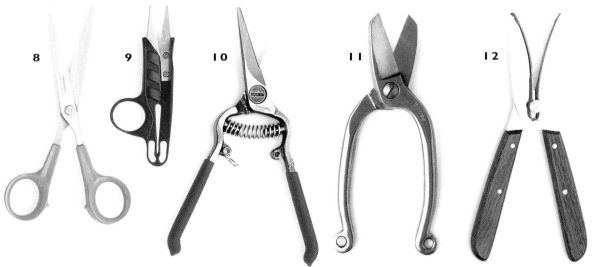

7 Billhook A billhook is used for heavy-duty cutting into woody growth, such as when coppicing hazel or laying a hedge. This example is double-edged, with a straight blade that can be used for chopping kindling wood. It has a 25cm forged-steel blade with a 15cm ash or hickory handle.

8 Household scissors Ordinary household scissors give a quick and crisp cut that is ideal for cutting chives or harvesting cut-and-come-again salads that regrow from a stump. Using scissors is much better than harvesting by hand, which tends to pull the young plants up. To keep the scissors clean, keep them in the kitchen rather than with other garden tools. These scissors are suitable for right- or left-handed use and are claimed to be dishwasher safe.

9 Floral clip An inexpensive multipurpose tool for making little snips in situations where scissors or hand pruners would be too big. For example, they are ideal for taking tip cuttings and trimming or deadheading small plants like houseplants, bedding cyclamen or alpines. They are not suitable for cutting woody stems. The tiny pointed blades are made of stainless steel and the handles are plastic.

10 Thinning shears The straight narrow blades of these shears reach into tight spaces without damaging the foliage or other plant tissue. Use them for light trimming and thinning of houseplants, and for general deadheading. The blunt tips make them suitable for grape thinning as they will not pierce the grapes. The forged coronium-steel alloy blades work with a scissor action and can be resharpened. These shears are suitable for both left and right handers.

11 Ikebana shears These beautifully shaped shears are designed for use in Japanese flower arranging (ikebana), but are useful for many types of cut flower, especially those with very sappy stems like daffodils and tulips. They are made of stainless steel and must be stored carefully as the blades do not close.

12 Cut-and-hold scissors A tool designed for cutting and holding flower stems. The stems are cut in the normal way but are held above the scissors by the strip of metal attached to the blades. Note that you have to hold the scissors with the metal attachment uppermost or it will not hold the cut stem. The piece of metal attached to the tip of the stainless-steel blade acts as a return spring. The scissors are light to hold, but if you have a weak grip, check that the spring action is not too tiring. These scissors are also useful for harvesting grapes.

Using cutting tools

Deadheading flowers If you want to prolong flowering, it is best to remove faded flowers promptly. Deadheading encourages the plant to divert its energy from seed production into producing more flowers. In the case of bulbs such as these daffodils, it helps the plants to remain full of vigour and to increase their clumps year by year. A few faded flower heads can simply be pinched off between finger and thumb, but if you have a lot of deadheading to do, it is quicker to use flower shears (or secateurs). These cut-and-hold scissors are handy for deadheading as they hold the faded flower.

Cut-and-come again salads and herbs By cutting off just the leaves you need for each meal and allowing the rest of the plant to grow on, you can produce a small but regular supply of fresh leaves in the tiniest space. Here a handful of chives is cut using household scissors. Holding the leaves in one hand, use a clean, sharp pair of scissors to cut the leaves. Cut right down to 2–3cm from the ground; if you simply snip the tips of the leaves, they will turn brown and look unsightly. Cutting is quick, and better than pulling leaves by hand, which can lift up young plants and expose their roots. A wide range of herbs and salads can be harvested in this way, including chervil, coriander, rocket and loose-leaf (not hearted) varieties of lettuce.

Training young trees There are several advantages to buying trees that are one or two years old and training them yourself. Apart from the cost saving, a young tree will invariably establish its roots quicker once it is planted in the ground, and so will soon catch up with an older tree that was planted at the same time. Training involves keeping the leading shoot straight by supporting it with a bamboo cane, cutting out any competing leading shoots with secateurs or a pruning knife, and removing the lower lateral shoots so a clear trunk can form. The laterals can be cut with secateurs, but if you have a lot of trees to train, a pruning knife is much quicker; this is what professionals use. Here a low lateral branch is removed from a young silver birch tree (*Betula pendula*), using a curved pruning knife.

supporting
and
training
plants

trellis, obelisks and frames

On a practical level, a trellis in a grid or latticework pattern provides support for climbing plants, but it can also add much to a garden in terms of decoration and screening. It is therefore worth using long-lasting trellis that suits the style of your house and garden. You may need to look further afield than your local garden centre and seek out specialist suppliers. If you plan to hire a designer, he or she will often design and commission trellis as part of the overall design. Trellis is traditionally made of rustic poles or planed timber, but there are now also metal, willow and bamboo designs.

Available in similar materials to trellis, obelisks are columns that narrow towards the top. As well as supporting plants, their strong vertical shapes make them instant focal points in a garden. Depending on their size, they are secured in place either by pushing their 'feet' into the ground or by using metal pegs. Some can be placed in containers such as Versailles planters.

Timber obelisks and trellis can be painted with a decorative paint or stain to harmonize with garden woodwork or to complement a plant colour.

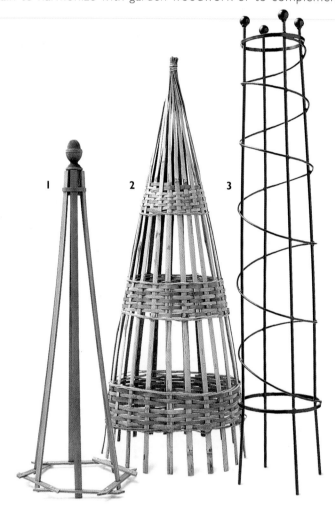

1 Container obelisk Useful in very small gardens, this wooden obelisk comes as a kit that is assembled and placed inside the rim of a container. It is available in two sizes: the smaller size fits containers with a diameter of 30–33cm; the larger fits pots of 35–60cm. Use it to support the less vigorous climbers such as large-flowered, summer-flowering clematis or black-eyed susan (*Thunbergia alata*).

2 Bamboo obelisk Obelisks woven from natural materials like bamboo and willow suit many garden styles, from cottage to contemporary, and are ideal for small potagers. They are a cheaper option than metal or wood versions, but not as long-lasting. To increase their lifespan, use them for annual climbers, such as climbing snapdragon (*Asarina antirrhiniflora*) or morning glory (*Ipomea*), so you can remove and store them under cover in winter.

3 Metal obelisk With its elegant spiral, this metal obelisk is decorative as well as practical. You could either use it for annual climbers such as sweet peas (*Lathyrus odoratus*), so it is left bare for winter interest, or grow perennials that are not too vigorous, such as climbing bellflower (*Codonopsis*), so it does not become totally masked. It is made from painted solid steel and supplied ready-assembled.

Topiary frames can be used to train suitable plants into definite shapes or as pruning guides for true box or yew topiary – when growth extends beyond the frame, trim the plant back into the desired shape. A ready-made frame like the ones featured is the ideal starting point for small projects like container topiary; for larger-scale projects, frames are usually made to order. The quickest results are achieved with 'false topiary', which involves training climbers or trailers such as ivy around a topiary frame. Frames made of wire mesh can also be filled with sphagnum moss and either left unplanted or planted with small-leaved ivy or creeping fig (*Ficus pumila*). The mesh needs to be wide enough to push the moss through but small enough to stop it coming out.

When buying a topiary frame, choose a material that will last the length of the project. Stainless steel or aluminium will last at least 20 years, so is suitable for large yew topiary. A cheaper alternative is to use a frame made of steel rods, dipped or sprayed with rust-proofing or paint.

With false or stuffed topiary animals, the outline becomes increasingly blurred once the plants establish, so look for a frame with sufficient detail, or the finished topiary will be unrecognizable.

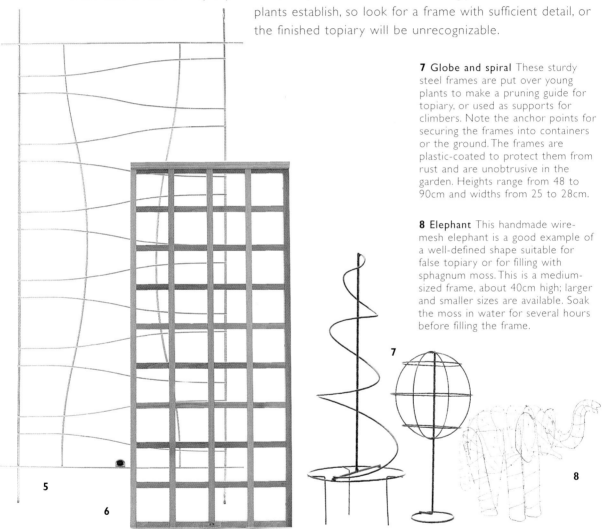

7 Globe and spiral These sturdy steel frames are put over young plants to make a pruning guide for topiary, or used as supports for climbers. Note the anchor points for securing the frames into containers or the ground. The frames are plastic-coated to protect them from rust and are unobtrusive in the garden. Heights range from 48 to 90cm and widths from 25 to 28cm.

8 Elephant This handmade wire-mesh elephant is a good example of a well-defined shape suitable for false topiary or for filling with sphagnum moss. This is a medium-sized frame, about 40cm high; larger and smaller sizes are available. Soak the moss in water for several hours before filling the frame.

4 Wooden obelisk Wooden obelisks are often made to order by local craftsmen, which can take several weeks, although it may be possible to have them painted a colour of your choice. This example comes as a kit, flat packed for ease of transport. It is easy to assemble, but you need to make sure the best side of the trellis is facing outwards when putting it together. Generous feet at the bottom allow the obelisk to be secured to the ground.

5 Metal trellis Ideal for a contemporary garden or the wall of a modern house, this sculptural metal trellis is made of rigid steel rods finished in zinc to reduce corrosion. Like most metal trellis, it takes up less ground space than wooden trellis because the metal rods are thinner than wooden battens. It is part of a modular system that can be joined together using special fixings to create screens; alternatively, the panels can be mounted on a wall.

6 Wooden trellis A classic, timeless style of trellis that will fit into many types of garden. This example is sturdy and well made, as the battens are thicker than many types of cheaper trellis. The timber is a naturally durable hardwood called iroko, which will mellow with age and needs no painting or preservative treatment. This means climbing plants can become established without disturbance.

Using plant supports

Even the smallest garden has room for an obelisk, a cane tripod or a trellis panel. On a practical level, they support climbing plants or wall shrubs with lax stems, such as ceanothus. In design terms, they lend structure and height to a garden. Trellis can be fixed to a wall using wooden battens or used with supporting posts to screen or enclose an area such as a patio, herb garden or vegetable plot. A single obelisk or tripod in a bed is a focal point; a pair can be used to mark an entrance. Placing supports in a row or in a geometric pattern gives a garden a formal touch.

The scale and position of obelisks and other supports are important. Before buying, it's worth experimenting by placing different lengths of bamboo canes in different parts of the garden. Note the heights and locations that work best.

Make sure vertical supports that are meant to be straight are truly straight by using a spirit level. Some are pushed into the ground, while others have a flat base that can be set on a concrete slab.

Most obelisks and sections of trellis are around 1.5–2m high, so choose a climber that is not too vigorous; most hardy annual climbers that grow to 2–3m are suitable, given that the growth twines around an obelisk or spreads out on a trellis panel.

The modern and miniature climbing roses that reach 2–3m, such as *Rosa* 'Warm Welcome' and 'Laura Ford', are ideal. They team up well with hybrid clematis such as *Clematis* 'Perle d'Azur' or the early flowering *C. alpina* or *C. macropetala* types.

Supports for hardy plants like roses need to be left out all year. Trellis or obelisks made of naturally durable wood such as teak or galvanized or plastic-coated metal are weatherproof and give the garden structure in winter. Supports for annual climbers can be set out in spring and taken under cover in autumn.

1 Sweet peas (*Lathyrus odoratus*) are the ideal climber for growing up a 2m painted wooden obelisk. Being hardy annuals, they are planted out in spring and discarded at the end of the season, giving access to remove, repaint or repair wooden support structures.

2 Once given a coating of lilac wood stain, a container obelisk makes an attractive support for this *Clematis* 'Edouard Desfossé', one of many early, large-flowered clematis cultivars that are ideal for containers.

3 Metal spirals give a sense of structure and a modern twist to an informal planting of white-flowered centaurea, stocks, *Salvia nemorosa*, violas and a hebe.

simple supports

A variety of different stakes, sticks and canes are used to support plants. Whether a tree needs staking or not depends on many factors: how windy the site is, the size and age of the tree, how it has been trained – if in doubt, ask when you buy the tree. Climbers and top-heavy herbaceous plants such as delphiniums need supporting either to prevent them collapsing, to improve the quality of crops or to display flowers better. What stakes you choose is a matter of personal preference. Some people believe supports should be hidden; others make a feature of them. Whatever you choose, make sure the support is in place early on, before the plant needs it – once a plant has grown top-heavy and fallen over, it is usually too late.

1 Pea sticks Traditionally used to support pea plants, birch twigs are also ideal for herbaceous border plants. Push the stems into the ground to form a circle around an emerging plant and bend the tops over into the centre to form a support. The plant will grow up to hide the supports. At the end of the season, pea sticks can be composted.

2 Hazel poles The coppicing of hazel to make poles is an old woodland craft that is enjoying a revival. The trimmed stems are used for growing climbers like runner beans. They are sturdier and more durable than pea sticks, but not as pliable.

3 Tree stake Not all trees need staking, but those that are 1.5m or over when planted will benefit from a stake in the early years as it anchors the plant and gives the roots time to establish. A stake need only be a third of the trunk height to be effective.

4 Bamboo canes Cheap, discreet and versatile, bamboo canes are classic items of gardening equipment. They are usually used to make wigwams, which are either tied at the top or held together with a special grip. Canes are sold in various lengths – shown here are 1m and 1.5m ones. To prolong the life of canes, store them in lengths of plastic drainpipe laid beside a shed.

5 Metal rods Longer-lasting versions of bamboo canes, these metal rods are coated with green plastic to make sturdy, unobtrusive plant supports. The ones shown are 1.4m and 1.8m long. The tops are moulded with plastic knobs to prevent eye injuries.

6 Terracotta finial A decorative version of a plastic cane grip, the terracotta finial will hold the tops of three canes to make a wigwam.

7 Split canes These thin green wood canes are ideal for supporting young or small plants. Use them for pot-grown species such as houseplants or fuchsia cuttings that will be trained into standards. Lengths range from 30cm to 75cm.

8 Cane caps It is important to cover the ends of canes in borders or vegetable plots to prevent nasty eye injuries, and few solutions are as elegant as these cane caps. Two types are shown here: the flat-topped ones are made of turned wood; those with curved tops are terracotta. Plastic versions are available.

9 Plastic cane grip This simple piece of plastic enables you to make a sturdy wigwam for sweet peas or runner beans in seconds. Up to seven bamboo canes can be held tightly in the holes.

10 Metal spiral This galvanized-steel spiral provides effective support for twining climbers and tomato plants. It is also attractive enough to be used unadorned as a piece of garden sculpture.

other supports

Most of these supports are for multi-stemmed plants. Some, like the link stakes and ring stakes, are used for herbaceous perennials, while the netting and wire provide a framework for climbers, cane fruits such as raspberries or wall shrubs like flowering quince (*Chaenomeles*) to spread horizontally on a wall or fence. Wires attached to posts can also be used to support rows of fruiting canes.

Netting is easier to use than wires in small spaces or for lightweight climbers such as annuals. Flexible netting is often used for annual or herbaceous climbers, and is removed and stored once the plants have died back.

Various metal stakes have been designed to support different herbaceous plants. They are useful for displaying the flowers of border plants and for keeping plants at the front of a border from flopping over onto a lawn or path.

1 Stiff netting This is tough polyethylene netting with a mesh size of 2cm. Attach it to fences, porches or arches to provide long-lasting support for climbers. It is rigid enough to be used as a low barrier, and can also be pegged down horizontally on a lawn to reduce wear and tear.

2 Flexible netting Thin but strong, this flexible netting is useful for lightweight climbers like sweet peas, garden peas and runner beans. The mesh size is 15cm, so this netting can also be used horizontally to support all the herbaceous plants in a border. To do this, use wooden stakes at each corner to support a raft of netting raised 45cm off the ground. Put the netting in place in late spring. By summer the plants will grow up through it and it will support them unseen.

3 Wire Galvanized wire of 10–14 gauge can be used to create long-term support along the length of a wall or fence. A series of parallel wires spaced 30–45cm apart are attached to the wall or fence with special fixings that hold them 5cm or so away from it. This makes it easy to tie the climbers in and allows air to circulate around them.

4 Tension bolts If horizontal wires on fence posts or freestanding posts are to extend more than 3m, it is best to use tension bolts to make sure they are taut. The wire is initially tightened by hand, then tightened further with the adjustable bolt.

5 Wall fixings These Italian wall fixings are easy to use and are an effective alternative to traditional vine eyes, which are hammered in. Use a drill with a masonry bit to make a hole for the rawlplug, then insert and twist the fixing until it is secure.

6 Loop stakes The circular loops can be attached to these metal stakes in a variety of ways. Shown here is a typical support suitable for a single-stemmed plant such as a lily or gladiolus.

7 Link stakes With this system, each stake links to the next to create a wide range of different shapes including squares, triangles and pentagons. The stakes can also be made into a straight line to restrain plants at the front of a border. Link stakes can be adapted to many different types of plants, and are quick to assemble and easy to store.

8 Ring stake This support is useful for multistemmed herbaceous plants like peonies. It is placed over an emerging plant that will grow through the circular grid and hide it. This example comes with a separate circular grid and three legs. It is preferable to a ready-joined version, which is awkward to store and often gets bent out of shape.

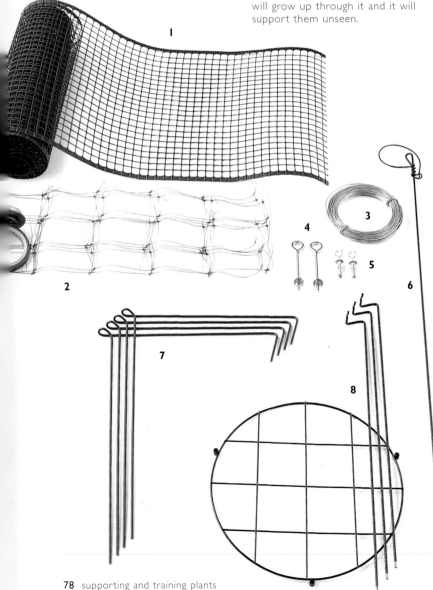

plant ties

Plant ties are needed to secure plants to their supports. The best tie for many herbaceous plants is simply raffia or a ball of soft, natural string. As well as being cheap and versatile, raffia and natural string are gentle on plant stems and will rot away after a couple of years. There are more permanent plant ties made of plastic or wire, but they need to be adjusted periodically to take account of stems thickening with age; otherwise the plant can be literally strangled to death.

For long-term plants such as staked trees or standard roses, it is best to use an easily adjustable tree tie made of rubber or plastic. The tie should be secure enough to hold the plant, but not tight against the stem. Again, it will need to be loosened as the girth of the stem increases.

1 Raffia This lightweight straw comes from a palm tree (*Raphia raffia*). It is easy to tie, surprisingly strong and like natural string it disintegrates after a couple of years so there is little risk of constricting plant stems. Raffia can be used for tying in most lightweight plants, and also for binding grafts. It is supplied in untidy bundles, so cut it into 10cm-long sections before you go out to tie plants.

2 Natural string Two- or three-ply string made from a natural material such as jute or coir (coconut fibres) is adequate for most lightweight tying jobs, such as tying climbers to their supports. The brown string shown here is made from coir and blends in well in a garden. Natural string lasts a couple of years, so is good for annuals, and can be used for longer-term plants as long as you re-tie them with new string. If held taut, it makes a simple vertical support; the fibrous texture encourages climbers to attach to it. To get the string really taut, soak it in water and work with it while wet; it then dries very tight.

3 Polypropylene twine This strong, rot-proof twine is best used for tying poles or canes together, or for attaching canes to wires when training climbers. If it is used to tie plants, it must be loosened and re-tied each year, or it will cut into the stems.

4 Velcro® Many areas of life have been made easier with Velcro fastenings, and tying plants is no exception. Velcro is particularly useful for anyone whose fingers are not as agile as they would like. Simply cut off a section, wrap it round the stem and its support, and press together. The strip shown is for tying herbaceous plants; Velcro also comes in a wider size, about 5cm, for tying trees.

5 Chainlink strap This soft material, with eyelets perforated along its length, is sold by the roll. Sections are cut off and secured by feeding the end through one of the eyelets. It can be used for almost any sized stem, and is easy to adjust. This is a cheap way of tying long-term plants.

6 Tree tie with buckle For securing a tree to a stake, use a strong, durable tree tie made of rubber or soft plastic. Choose one with a buffer to separate the stake from the stem and prevent chafing. Adjust the tie with the buckle as the tree grows.

7 Supersoft tree tie This is a strong but soft alternative to a tree tie with a buckle. If you find buckles hard to undo, moving the eyelet along the notched tie might be an easier option.

8 Rose tie This simple plastic buckle tie with a collar is just the right size for securing standard roses to stakes.

9 Plastic ties These thin, adjustable ties are used for attaching lightweight plants to canes. Notches are passed through an eyelet to secure the tie. Ties can be used separately or joined together, and are useful if you have lots of stems to tie in, for example if you grow rows of fruit canes.

10 Plant rings These plastic-coated metal rings are an alternative to plastic ties. They can be opened and closed easily, and are used for securing lightweight stems to bamboo canes or split canes.

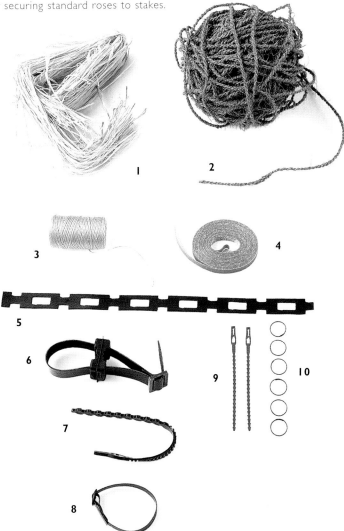

Planting and staking a tree

Trees of 1.5m or more when planted will benefit from staking in their first couple of years. The stake should be put in place at the time of planting – after digging the hole but before putting in the tree – to avoid damaging the roots. Stakes can usually be removed after a couple of years, although standard roses, weeping standards and top-grafted trees need permanent staking because they become top-heavy.

1 Dig a hole twice the size of the rootball. Use a mallet to hammer a wooden stake into the hole, positioning it just off centre for a container-grown tree, but right in the centre for a bare-rooted tree. If the tree's rootball is so large that you cannot place a vertical stake close enough to the tree, insert a short stake further away and lean it at a 45-degree angle towards the tree. Position the stake so it leans into the prevailing wind.

2 Remove the tree from its pot or sacking, and position it in the ground so that it is at the same level it was in the container or nursery bed; lay a cane across the hole to check the level. Fill the hole with the original soil mixed with a soil improver such as garden compost. You may need to tie the stem to the stake with some raffia to keep it in place while filling the hole. Firm the soil with your foot.

3 As the tree grows, its girth will increase, so use an adjustable tree tie that can be loosened to prevent damage. Buckle tree ties often have a buffer between the stake and the tree to protect the bark from friction damage. Fit the tie and nail it to the stake. Here a bamboo cane has been inserted next to the stem because the tree's leading shoot had been damaged. The cane will be removed once a new leading shoot has been trained.

Supporting perennials

Perennials like the taller delphiniums need staking to display their flower spikes to best effect and to prevent them from collapsing after summer rain. Put the supports in place by late spring – at this time you can see the extent of the emerging growth, but it is still low enough for you to move around the border easily without damaging it. Choose a day when the soil is moist to make it easier to insert the supports.

  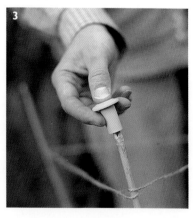

1 Encircle the emerging clump of perennial foliage with three or four bamboo canes. Keeping the canes straight, push each one 10–15cm into the ground. If the ground is too hard to take the canes, make a hole with a poker or metal rod first, otherwise the canes will break. When pushing a cane into the ground, support the middle section with both hands to prevent it from snapping.

2 Once the canes have been inserted around the clump, take a ball of garden string and tie one end securely (with a double knot) to the bottom of one of the canes. Wind the string around each cane to form an enclosure, then tie it onto the original one. Repeat this process at intervals up the canes. Three circles of string equally spaced along the canes is usually sufficient. The string should be taut.

3 One drawback of hidden supports is that the ends can cause serious eye injuries either to gardeners bending down to cultivate plants or to children retrieving balls from borders. Always put some form of eye protector over garden canes. You can improvise with corks or empty film canisters, but as the tops of the canes are usually visible, it is worth buying special cane caps.

protecting plants

cold frames, cloches and forcing pots

The items featured here will give plants a little extra cosseting in order to produce earlier flowers or, in the case of forcing pots, protect tender crops. While none of these products is essential, they provide an extra couple of weeks of growing time at the start and end of the growing season, which for a keen gardener can be invaluable.

Glass has a long tradition as a plant protector. The word 'cloche' comes from the French for bell, and refers to the glass bells made by glass blowers from about 1630 onwards for protecting crops. Modern alternatives to glass, such as polycarbonate, are worth considering where safety and ease of assembly and storage are priorities. As well as the structural items shown here, there are also sheets of material that can be used as weather protectors, such as garden fleece (see page 86).

The purpose of a cloche is to warm the soil and surrounding air so that early sowings or young plants stand a better chance of germinating and establishing at the start of the growing season. They are used mainly for cropping plants and are moved to another row once the first row has got going. A good cloche should stay put (the light ones have tendency to blow away), allow quick access so you can check the plants and be easy to move around. In reality, few cloches are perfect in every respect, so you will have to compromise, although the ones shown here are better than most.

A cold frame provides a halfway house for young plants in spring when they have to make the transition between the warmth of the indoors and the cooler conditions outdoors. Plants need 10–14 days to acclimatize themselves in a cold frame, first with the lid on, but later with the lid open during the day and on at night, until they can be left with the lid off. Cold frames are usually glazed and have a wood or aluminium frame. They resemble mini-greenhouses, which is perhaps not surprising as they are made by greenhouse manufacturers.

On a warm day, a cloche or cold frame can be a death trap for young plants or seedlings as so much heat is trapped inside them, so proper ventilation, which can be easily adjusted as the weather changes, is essential.

A forcing pot has a similar shape to a bell jar, but its function is very different. Being opaque, a forcing pot not only brings growth on early, but deprives the plant of light. Lack of light leads to the 'blanching' of leaves and stems, which reduces stringiness and bitterness in crops such as rhubarb and seakale. Made of terracotta, forcing pots have great decorative value in a kitchen garden.

I

I Cold frame
This simple wooden cold frame is quick to assemble and dismantle, thanks mainly to the polycarbonate lids. There are two lids, which can be lifted off if necessary. Most cold frames have hinged lids, but removable ones are less likely to get damaged by the wind. Softwood frames like this pine one are less expensive than hardwood, but are more prone to rot if wet. To prolong the life of a cold frame, set it on slabs or gravel rather than placing it on bare earth. This frame is 107cm long, 66cm wide and 46cm high.

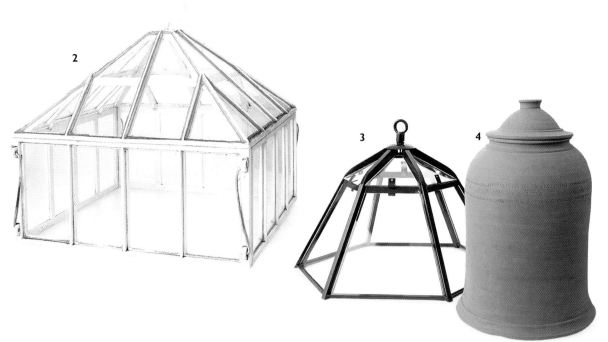

2 Square lantern cloche This is a reproduction of a classic Victorian cloche with a cast-iron frame and glass sides held in place by putty. The heavy structure will stand up to wind and makes an attractive feature in a vegetable bed. The base is 55 x 55cm, so there is enough ground space for rows of young salad plants or herbs, and at around 60cm high there is plenty of headroom, too.

3 Round lantern cloche One of the most decorative types of cloche, a lantern cloche will greatly enhance a potager or ornamental kitchen garden. This design is based on a traditional French cloche, but with several improvements: the painted aluminium frame makes it lightweight, yet strong and stylish, and the glass sides are held in place with metal clips rather than putty, so they can be removed for ventilation or storage.

4 Forcing pot This terracotta forcing pot is beautifully shaped and ideal for a potager or for forcing seakale or rhubarb growing in a border. The lid allows you to check the progress of the plant without lifting the whole pot. This example is 50cm high and is sold as a seakale forcer, but pots of this size are tall enough for rhubarb and may be considerably cheaper than taller pots sold as rhubarb forcers.

5 Row cloche Serious vegetable growers will value this cloche for its useful tunnel shape. It covers a row of plants and gives them more headroom than a tent-shaped cloche. The legs are easy to push into the ground, and the metal frame makes it stable enough to be moved around, although the flimsy end pieces tend to fall out when you pick it up. The row cloche is 122cm long, 45cm wide and 40cm high.

6 Bell jar A modern version of the traditional blown-glass bell jar. Made of thin plastic, it is cheaper, lighter and safer than the real thing. There are holes in the rim through which 16cm metal pegs can be pushed to secure the cloche to the ground. Using the pegs as supports, it can also be raised off the ground if necessary for ventilation. The cloche is 26cm high and 34cm in diameter. There is a larger version for protecting tender shrubs or perennials.

7 Polycarbonate cloche This lightweight cloche can be slotted together in seconds, and it stores flat. Metal pegs are supplied to secure it to the ground, but the really neat part of the design is that it opens from the top, allowing you to check on the progress of young plants and water them without removing the pegs. The cloche is 60cm long, 40cm wide and 35cm high.

Using plant protectors

I Forcing rhubarb For an early crop of tender rhubarb, cover a dormant clump in midwinter with a forcing pot. The pot will keep out the light, and the stems will be blanched pink. Check the crop's progress by lifting the lid of the pot. Eventually, the new growth will push the lid off. The rhubarb can be harvested in early to mid spring: remove the forcing pot, then pull, rather than cut, the stems. Cut off the leaves, which are poisonous.

2 Improving germination Broad beans are hardy, but need a minimum temperature of 5°C to germinate, so two weeks before the first sowing put a cloche over the ground to warm the soil and increase the germination rate. A tunnel cloche such as this is ideal for a double row of broad beans.

3 Producing an early crop This early sowing of leafy salad and herbs is growing well, thanks to the warmth provided by a square lantern cloche. The lid has been set at an angle to encourage air to circulate, which will prevent fungal disease. The cloche is being used to protect plants growing in a wooden raised bed, a combination that also minimizes slug damage.

Tools for a productive garden

By promoting the importance of using only the best, locally produced ingredients, Darina Allen has transformed the image of Irish food. A broadcaster and author of many cookery books, she also runs, with her husband Timmy, the Ballymaloe Cookery School at Kinoith in County Cork. The grounds have extensive fruit, herb and vegetable gardens (see opposite), which supply the needs of both the cookery school and the nearby Ballmaloe House Hotel and Restaurant. Here Darina describes how she uses cloches and other tools to grow top-quality produce all year round.

'My favourite gardening tool is a cloche. The ones I use were made by my son Isaac, who modelled them on Victorian originals by making a metal frame and fitting it with glass. These cloches are very ornamental, which is important as we like the kitchen garden to be decorative as well as productive. They help to bring on early crops such as leafy salads and to prolong the harvest of late ones like peppers and chilies. I find them invaluable in spring when young plants raised in the greenhouse are moved to the kitchen garden. The shelter they provide allows plants to be gradually acclimatized to the outdoor conditions, and this gives them a good start. As the weather gets warmer, it is worth rotating the top of the cloche to improve air circulation within, and so prevent overheating. The cloches are moved around the kitchen garden as required, the priority being to give protection to crops that might be a bit tender when first planted out, such as bush tomatoes. Sweet peppers and chillies normally crop better under glass than in the open garden. However, as they are small plants, they can remain under the cloche all through the growing season, which is an effective way of improving the yield of tasty ripe fruits. Another tool that is both ornamental and functional is the forcing pot. I use terracotta ones with lids for getting seakale to produce tender succulent white shoots.'

sheet materials

The use of synthetic sheet materials such as garden fleece to guard against the vagaries of the weather has revolutionized commercial horticulture, and these advances are now trickling down to amateur gardeners. Featured here is a selection of the most useful available.

Most of these materials are available in packs from garden centres, or are sold on rolls, so you can purchase them by the metre. Garden fleece is now also sold ready sewn into a tube, which makes it easier to use. If you need large quantities of any type of material, savings can often be made by buying from mail-order horticultural suppliers. A recent trend is for sheet materials to be sold with fixings or pegs. To cut the size of sheet you want, use a large pair of household scissors. A sharp knife can be used for cutting lengths of polythene or making slits to plant through.

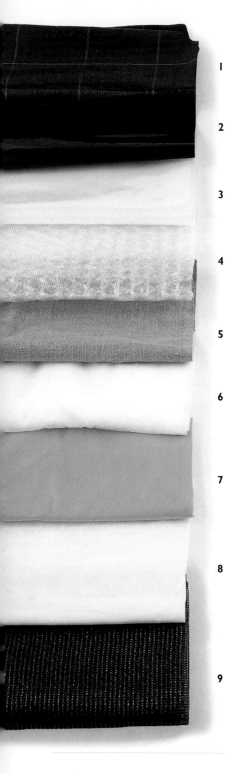

1 Sheet mulch Laying a sheet mulch in a border in spring before planting will help plants to establish quicker and survive dry spells, and reduces the need for watering and weeding. The mulch can also be used on paths or under gravel. Permeable mulches such as the woven polypropylene shown are superior to non-permeable ones as they let water and air through to the soil. The grid lines are for measuring out the fabric and spacing plants. To join sheets together, overlap and pin them down with metal pegs.

2 Black polythene Heavy-duty black polythene is a cheap alternative to sheet mulch where large areas need to be covered, such as when bringing land into cultivation, or growing rows of strawberries or potatoes. Puddles of water collect on the surface, so puncture drainage holes with a fork or lay the sheet over a ridge of earth so the water drains off.

3 Clear polythene Polythene can be draped over a row of metal hoops to make an inexpensive cloche. Setting up a clear polythene barrier, at least 75cm high, around carrots will block the path of carrot fly and prevent crop damage. Offcuts can be used to line raised beds or containers, but remember to make drainage holes.

4 Bubble insulation To reduce greenhouse heating bills, line the inside of the glass with bubble insulation; use drawing pins on a wooden frame and special plastic fixings if the frame is aluminium. The insulation shown, with large bubbles in clear plastic sheeting, is the most efficient insulator; sheets with smaller bubbles, used for packaging, are not as effective. Bubble insulation can also be used for cold frames, compost bins and containers.

5 Hessian This natural material has much to offer as an insulator as it is less noticeable in the garden than most synthetic materials and can be recycled. Use a double layer packed with straw or bracken to insulate tender evergreens, or tack a sheet to wooden battens fixed to a wall to protect wall plants of borderline hardiness. Squares of hessian can be used to wrap bare-rooted plants so they don't dry out.

6 White fleece This is the easiest frost protector to use, being lighter and safer than glass, and adapting to any shape that needs protection. Fleece will also protect plants from wind, hail and flying pests. It can be draped over metal hoops to make a tunnel or simply laid lightly over the plants. Fleece is best removed once all danger of frost has passed as plants underneath it can overheat in warm weather. It is made from spun polypropylene fibres and is available in different thickness; the more expensive thicker types provide more frost protection and last longer, but they transmit less light. As fleece is a very lightweight fabric, it must be well secured to the ground with special pegs (see below), bricks or large stones, otherwise the benefits will be lost. Thick fleece (30 grams) is suitable for insulating a greenhouse. Dirty fleece can be washed in a washing machine.

7 Green fleece This variation on basic white fleece can be used to shade or insulate a greenhouse; special clips can be bought to hold it in place. It is not suitable for laying over growing plants.

8 Dot-matrix shading A state-of-the-art shading material that clings to clean glass and polycarbonate surfaces by static electricity, so avoiding the need for time-consuming fixings or adhesives. Like all shading materials, it is most effective when applied outside the glass.

9 Knitted polyethylene Lightweight and easy to handle, this material can be used for shading or to protect plants from wind and hail. It is also used to make storage bags for vegetables and bulbs.

10 Pegs Most sheet materials need to be held firmly in place or they will blow away. Use these plastic pegs for securing the edges of fleece to the ground.

Protection from cold winds

Young evergreen shrubs and semi-tender shrubs like myrtles, cordylines and phormiums are worth wrapping up for the coldest months. Those in small containers can often be moved undercover over winter, but this is not practical for large specimens, which are best protected in situ.

1 This large cordyline makes an impressive container plant but is now too big to move into a greenhouse in winter. To protect the plant from cold winds, gather up the foliage and tie it with elastic bands or strips of hessian. Cover the plant with an insulating material such as garden fleece; the type featured here is sold as a tube, which means it is easily slipped over shrubs.

2 Even if they are hardy, container-grown plants can be damaged if their rootball freezes. In cold weather, wrap the sides of the container with a double layer of bubble insulation, but leave a small gap at the top so you can check whether the compost needs watering later. Once the worst of the frosts are over, remove the bubble insulation and unwrap the fleece.

Hardening off

Plants that have been raised in a greenhouse (or purchased in the covered areas of a garden centre) need to be acclimatized gradually to outdoor conditions before planting. This process is called hardening off, and it usually takes 10–14 days. During this period, garden fleece will protect the plants from extremes of temperature.

1 Bring the plants outside 10–14 days before planting out, and place in a warm sheltered spot. Lay a sheet of fleece over young plants during the day. Take the plants back indoors at night. After 6 days or so, depending on the weather, keep the fleece off in mild spells during the day, but put on a double layer at night.

2 Secure the edges of the fleece firmly to the ground using special fleece pegs or bricks. Top-quality fleece can be washed in the washing machine and re-used several times. It is possible to buy fleece with a reinforced edge, which will last longer and is easier to secure at the edges.

protection from animals

Putting up a barrier around plants is one of the most effective – and environmentally friendly – methods of protecting them against garden pests. A few barriers provide some protection against wind as well. Most of these items are needed only when the plants are young, or in the case of fruit, while they are cropping.

Barriers are a gardener's main preventative measure against birds and the larger mammals like rabbits and squirrels. A barrier should be installed before any major damage can occur, and must be secure, particularly if it will be used over the winter months when wind and snow could dislodge it. Check the barrier regularly for holes and repair them promptly. Netting is often draped over plants and left loose at the edges, which means that birds and other pests can still reach the crop. Stretch the netting over a wooden frame and secure the edges well. If you have the space, the ultimate in fruit protection is a walk-in cage, which can provide a permanent barrier for a wide range of crops.

1 Chicken wire Galvanized wire netting makes a tough barrier that will keep out rabbits, squirrels and birds. It can be attached to wooden posts inserted around plants or a wooden frame. The mesh diameter is 13mm.

2 Pond netting This plastic netting, with a mesh of 18mm, is fairly stiff so it will not sag when used to cover a pond. It can also be fixed to a wooden frame to make a fruit cage.

3 Fine mesh A boon to organic vegetable growers, this fine-gauge plastic mesh will keep out small flying pests such as cabbage-white butterflies and carrot flies, so there is no need to spray crops with chemicals. A series of galvanized metal hoops over a bed can be used to support fleece early in the season; once this is removed, the fine mesh can take its place. The mesh need not be removed to water the plants growing under it.

4 Fruit netting This flexible, expandable plastic netting is draped over bamboo canes topped with inverted pots to protect individual fruit bushes such as redcurrants or strawberry plants from bird damage. The mesh has a diameter of 10mm.

5 Bark wrap Protect the bark of young trees from being nibbled by rabbits with this simple plastic wrap. The loose spiral of plastic expands as the girth of the stem increases.

6 Stem guard Anyone who uses a power trimmer to cut grass around a young tree should fit one of these protective guards to protect the bark from damage. Simply open up the curved plastic and slip it around the stem.

7 Shrub shelter An idea taken from forestry and amenity horticulture, this shelter, made of correx, is inexpensive and will greatly improve the chances of survival of a young tree or shrub. It provides protection from small animals such as rabbits and squirrels, and from wind and herbicide damage for the growing season after planting. A stake can be inserted inside to give more stability.

8 Domes These structures are more attractive than most barriers and will protect young plants or emerging perennials from cats, birds and ball games. The examples shown here are made from willow (above) and bamboo (below). Both need to be secured to the ground with metal pegs. Various sizes are available, from 30 to 75cm diameter.

containers

small pots

We have defined a small pot as one that is under 30cm in diameter. For many plants, such as bedding and smaller herbs, pots of this size will be their final destination. For larger perennials or shrubs, the pots will be temporary homes, and further repotting will be needed as the plants grow. In this case, choose a pot that is wider at the top so the rootball can be extracted easily.

As design tools, small pots offer great flexibility for creating and changing container displays. They can be used individually, for example as a centrepiece on a garden table, or grouped together in single- or mixed-species displays on a shelf or along the top of a low wall. They are also good for using on steps as they leave enough space for people to walk by safely. As they are easy to move around, small pots are the best choice for frequently changing displays, such as a group of bulbs, or for herbs that you might want to move from outdoors to indoors.

Wall planters are specially shaped so that they can be hung flat on a wall. They are ideal for enlivening featureless expanses of wall belonging to the house or an outbuilding, or around a patio.

Designing with small pots

O Use small pots to display a collection of spring bulbs, auriculas, perlargoniums, cacti or herbs. For greater impact, group them on a display bench or staging, or on a shelf in a conservatory or greenhouse.

O Use a line of pots, equally spaced and potted with the same plant, to enhance linear features such as paths, steps or the edges of patios and decks.

O Wall planters filled with trailing plants add lushness to a patio or enclosed seating area. Position several of the same style either in a line or in a triangle across the wall and fill with the same plants.

1 Terracotta flowerpots The classic terracotta flowerpot fits into any garden style. The tapering shape allows for easy repotting and for stacking pots that are not in use. The thick rim makes them easy to grip and carry. These pots are available in a wide range of sizes, allowing regular potting-on of plants as they grow. Shown here are 10cm, 20cm and 30cm diameter pots.

2 Terracotta long tom These deep pots were originally made for plants that resent root disturbance, but are often used to display trailing plants such as small-leaved ivies or *Lotus berthelotii*. You may see pots of a more exaggerated shape than this one, but they are not always stable.

3 Shallow terracotta pot Also known as half-pots or alpine pans, these are ideal for shallow-rooting plants like small bulbs, succulents, alpines, houseleeks (*Sempervivum*) and many small herbs such as thymes. They can also be grouped with taller containers to anchor a display visually.

4 Plastic pot Plastic pots are much more cost-effective than terracotta versions, for example if you want a large number for growing vegetables or salads, or want to move bulbs in pots around the garden. At 30cm in diameter, this one is the ideal size for growing vegetables on a patio.

Material choice Terracotta, which means 'baked earth', is the classic choice for outdoor containers. It has a natural texture, ages gracefully and fits into almost any garden style. However, the quality of the clay used to make terracotta pots varies greatly. Being porous, terracotta absorbs moisture, and at freezing point the water expands, causing the pots to flake or shatter. Pots that are to be left outside in winter need to have been fired at a very high temperature to reduce their porosity. They are more expensive and are guaranteed frost-proof (nearly all pots are sold as being 'frost resistant', which is a pretty meaningless claim). Another option is to use glazed terracotta pots. The glaze makes them less porous, but the glazing often develops fine cracks in winter.

Plastic pots have improved greatly in recent years, and they are worth considering if you need to buy a lot of pots cheaply or if the location requires lightweight containers, for example a balcony or roof garden. Choose pots with simple shapes and natural colours that are made of thick, good-quality plastic such as polypropylene. The cheaper, thinner plastic tends to go brittle and break. The drawbacks with plastic are that the roots can overheat in hot weather and there is more risk of waterlogging in winter.

Metal pots in square or rectangular shapes suit contemporary outdoor spaces. Galvanized for protection against rust, they are durable over winter, and unlike other materials, they do not go brittle, chip or crack. However, they will not insulate the rootball against extremes of temperature, so use a mulch of pebbles, gravel or glass beads, or position them away from direct sun.

5   6   7

5 Terrazzo pot Used as a cool flooring material in Mediterranean villas, terrazzo is made by mixing fine marble chips with concrete, then wet polished to give it a sleek, smooth feel. Terrazzo pots are available in white or grey, and look chic filled with single species, even humble plants such as marigolds. They do not have drainage holes.

6 Glazed pots Glazing terracotta makes it less porous, so it will not dry out as readily and there is less

risk of frost damage. Glazed pots are very variable – even pots from the same batch will be slightly different, reflecting their positions in the kiln or slight impurities in the raw materials. It is therefore worth checking each pot when buying to select a finish you like. This applies particularly to pots with metallic glazes, such as the spherical pot shown; these glazes can be either very shiny or slightly matt.

7 Metal pot Filled with small grasses or herbs such as chives, basil or parsley, a line of these contemporary aluminium pots looks great on steps or a garden table, or on a windowsill indoors. The thick sides make them more robust and a better environment for plant roots than the cheaper, thinner metal pots. Metal pots are often sold without drainage holes, so it is essential to put in a generous layer of gravel before adding the compost, and to avoid overwatering.

8   9   10

8 Glazed wall pot The low porosity of glazed terracotta makes it a good material for a planter on a sunny wall, where a small volume of compost is more vulnerable to drying out. Glazed terracotta still has a cooling effect on roots, giving it an advantage over plastic or polythene-lined wicker pots.

9 Wicker wall pot Rustic wicker wall pots are ideal for cottage gardens. They are lined with polythene to conserve moisture and to prolong their life. Cut drainage holes in the bottom of the liner before planting. Wicker pots are best used for annuals and brought indoors in winter.

10 Plastic wall pot Made to look like terracotta embossed with a motif, this plastic planter is perfect for a Mediterranean-style patio. Plastic's tendency to become waterlogged or overheated can be overcome to some extent by choosing a larger planter with a greater volume of compost.

large pots and urns

Large pots, defined here as being over 30cm in diameter, can create much more impact in a garden than smaller ones, and are easier to maintain. This is because the greater volume of compost acts as a buffer, protecting the roots from extremes of temperature and moisture. A useful diameter is 45cm, which is suitable for a small tree or shrub or a mixed planting of perennials, bulbs and annuals.

Large pots are much more expensive than smaller ones, especially terracotta, so choose for the long term. Strongly patterned or brightly coloured pots are eye-catching, but make sure they will fit in with the style of your garden and ask yourself if you will find them attractive in a year's time. If in doubt, choose classic shapes and neutral colours such as whites and greys that will work with any shade of flower or foliage. A mulch of glass pebbles, gravel or shells can be used to add interest.

When choosing a large pot, consider the size in relation to the setting. A pot that is in scale with the garden and other features around it will create a harmonious, balanced effect. Alternatively, you could break the rules and use an oversize pot or urn in a small space to create a dramatic focal point. As large pots are prominent, long-term features, it is worth sketching them on a scale drawing of the garden or using canes to rig up a model in order to work out the best size and location. Take a tape measure with you when buying pots as the size is not always given.

A single large pot or an urn on a pedestal creates a focal point at the end of a vista or in the middle of a courtyard, while a pair of large pots can be used to flank an entrance or the top of a flight of steps. A cluster of different-sized pots works well in the corner of a patio.

1 Plastic tub This is one of the best large plastic pots, with a diameter of 50cm. It is a good alternative to a wooden barrel as it needs less maintenance and is easier to move around, using the discrete handles. The neutral grey colour blends in well with most schemes. Made of polypropylene, it will give many years of service without becoming brittle. This is a versatile container that can be used for aquatic-style plantings, using small waterlilies, for example, or, if drainage holes are made in the base, for single small trees or shrubs or mixed plantings of perennials, annuals and bulbs. The volume of compost is also large enough to support several potato plants or, with suitable support, a dwarf runner bean such as 'Hestia'.

2 Glazed ceramic pot A large glazed pot with several worthwhile features. The glaze extends up and over the entire rim, which will give an attractive, finished look to a planting, particularly if low-growing plants are used to underplant a taller one. The shape and thickness of the pot ensure that top-heavy plantings, such as a small shrub or tree, are stable. Glazed pots set off ornamental grasses and other foliage plants, such as Japanese maples and dwarf pines, to good effect. The pot has a diameter of 45cm.

3 Large terracotta pot With a maximum diameter of 45cm, this elegant flared pot offers plenty of room for underplanting a central plant. The basket-weave pattern adds texture and will make an effective contrast with small, airy flowers like marguerites. The colour of terracotta works well with pink roses, or with the hot reds of pelargoniums.

4 Fibreglass pot Like plastic, fibreglass is lightweight and frost-resistant, and can be moulded into different shapes. However, it is available in a much wider range of finishes, including copper, bronze, lead, weathered terracotta and stone. Pots with good-quality finishes are expensive, but they are fairly durable. This stylish copper-blue pot is one of a series entitled 'Bell Jars', designed by sculptor Bill Harling. It comes in several sizes; this one has a diameter of 50cm.

5 Fibreglass urn and pedestal The classic shape of this urn looks elegant even when empty, but fill it with trailing plants and a central architectural species, such as a cordyline, and you will have a stunning feature for very little effort. This version is made of fibreglass finished to look like stone. As well as being much cheaper, fibreglass urns are lighter and come in a wider range of finishes. They are often sold without drainage holes, so these need to be drilled around the bottom of the bowl. The urn has a diameter of 50cm, and the combined height of the urn and pedestal is 108cm.

6 Cast-stone bowl and urn Cast-stone containers are made by pouring crushed stone and concrete into moulds. If hand-finished like these, the result looks like sculpted stone. The colour and finish can be chosen to match architectural features of the house or garden. As well as these contemporary designs, ornate Victorian or Italianate styles are available. Cast stone is porous and, left in a damp, shady place, will soon age attractively as lichen and moss colonize the surface. These are heavy items that are best left in situ. They are frostproof, but their porosity means there is a risk of winter damage in very cold climates. The containers shown here come with a 25-year guarantee against frost damage. The diameter of the bowl is 52cm, and that of the urn is 48cm.

5

4

7 Angle-top pot Containers with angled tops draw the eye into the pot and offer a different perspective on the plants within. When finishing off the planting, make sure the surface of the compost mirrors the angle of the pot. Such pots offer plenty of scope for underplanting with spring bulbs, alpines or bedding plants. Alternatively, use a mulch of pebbles or gravel to set off an evergreen shrub or small tree. Angle-top pots are available in plain or glazed terracotta, and in various sizes and shapes.

6

7

Planting a large pot

Waterlogging can be fatal to container-grown plants, so good drainage is essential. Custom-made terracotta or glazed pots have drainage holes, but you may need to drill holes in plastic, wood or fibreglass containers. Put the pot in its final position before planting. Water the plant well before preparing the pot.

1 Cover the base of the pot with a layer of crocks (bits of broken clay pots) or large stones, and cover this with a layer of gravel. Add enough compost so the plant will be at the same level in the new pot as it was in the old one. Potting or multipurpose compost is suitable for most plants, but acid-loving species such as azaleas and citrus fruits should be grown in a lime-free (ericaceous) compost. Composts based on peat, coir or bark are lighter in weight, while loam-based ones are heavier. The compost can be mixed with topsoil, leafmould or garden compost, but it is best to cover it with a layer of potting compost to prevent weeds.

2 Tip the plant out of the existing pot. If the roots have been encircling the pot, tease them out gently with your fingers. Place the plant in its new pot, making sure the plant is level. Pack fresh compost around the roots and the sides of the container and firm it down gently with your hands, leaving a 3cm gap between the surface of the compost and the rim of the pot to make watering easier.

3 Underplant with smaller plants or add a 3cm layer of mulch to the surface of the compost to help retain moisture and prevent weeds (the compost surface will need to be 3cm lower to retain a 3cm gap).

Successful container gardening

Ken Druse is an award-winning author and photographer, and is the Gardening Editor of America's House Beautiful magazine. He has been described as the founder of the natural gardening movement in America, which stresses the importance of taking the ecology of plants into account when using them in the garden, and his books on the subject have an enthusiastic following. He is a keen container gardener, and here he shares some of his secrets for success.

'Planting a large pot is just like planting a border. Start with a tall architectural plant and fill in with smaller subjects, perhaps a medium-sized plant for volume, then a groundcover species to drape over the sides of the pot (for an example of this, see opposite). If you have a really big, attractively shaped pot, it is also worth asking yourself whether it needs plants in it at all – if well positioned, many look great left empty.

A favourite trick is to plant individual plants in their own small pots and to cluster the pots together to make an impressive display. This allows you to have a moveable feast – once the blooms have faded on a plant, the pot can be whipped away and another one with a fresh display brought in to fill the space.

A mistake made by many people is to plant containers so they look great all at once – in spring, for example; such displays soon run out of steam before the end of the growing season. As well as planting containers in spring, I also plant them on the 4th of July to provide displays that last until autumn.

I like using artificial terracotta pots made of plastic as they retain moisture better than the real thing. A neat tip is to sandpaper the seam left from the mould to make them look more realistic. Plastic pots are also easier to move under cover in winter. Here in New York the winters can be severe and even good-quality concrete pots can erode badly. To prevent this, I turn empty pots upside down or cover them with insulating plastic.'

planters and troughs

Square or rectangular planters and troughs offer an alternative to circular pots and are particularly useful in areas that are defined by the straight lines or corners of architecture, such as courtyards, patios, decks, porches, balconies and roof gardens.

Wood is a commonly used material for planters and troughs as it is can be adapted to suit different garden styles. Rough or recycled timber is appropriate for a natural or country garden, while planed timber, which is often painted or stained, is in keeping with town gardens or formal styles. A wooden planter will require some maintenance, although lining the inside with polythene or using a stiff liner made of fibreglass or recycled paper will help prevent moisture rotting the sides. A painted or stained wooden planter must be kept looking smart with a fresh lick of paint or stain every other year or so. To reduce maintenance, choose planters made of a naturally durable hardwood such as oak or teak, or opt for good-quality plastic, fibreglass or galvanized metal, depending on your garden's style.

A pair of square planters, perhaps filled with topiary or a standard rose, can be used to mark an entrance or a garden bench. A square planter fitted with an obelisk (see page 74) makes an attractive container for a climbing rose or a clematis. The original Versailles planter was a wooden box especially made for plants that spent the summer on the terrace of the palace and the winter in the orangery. Today the style is reproduced in many materials and used for both tender and hardy plants.

Troughs resemble windowboxes, but are usually longer and deeper and are used on the ground in areas where there is no open soil, such as where a paved surface meets a wall, or on a balcony. They are deep enough to use for perennials, small shrubs or climbers. Climbers need the support of a trellis that is either mounted on the wall or attached to the container.

Like large pots, planters and troughs are long-term features in the garden, and many are difficult to move once planted, so choose and position them with care.

1 Versailles planter This top-of-the-range example of a classic planter is made of oak that has been given an oil finish. It is 45cm square and comes with a fibreglass lining so you need to drill drainage holes through the lining and the planter. There are many other versions of these smart planters, and the wood can be stained or painted to coordinate with the planting or with woodwork around the house or garden.

2 Fibreglass planter For a container that requires no maintenance and is easy to move from indoors to outdoors, consider a fibreglass planter. The range of finishes gives plenty of scope for matching your interior decor. This one has a wheatsheaf motif and a verdigris finish. There are no drainage holes, and these need to be drilled if you want to use it outside only. If you want to have the option of moving the planter indoors, you could leave it intact and insert a liner with drainage holes so water does not drip on the floor.

1

2

3 Wooden trough A substantial six-sided wooden trough that can be used on its own against a wall or as part of a modular system of decking, seating and arches. Well-built and stable, it takes a large volume of compost, so is suitable for long-term plants such as climbers and shrubs.

4 Plastic trough Ideal for balconies or roof gardens, this lightweight plastic trough could be used for seasonal fillers such as bedding, or to grow a mixture of salad crops or other quick-growing vegetables like carrots or radish. It is one of the better-quality plastic troughs with a double thickness of curved plastic at the top to reduce the likelihood of buckling. It is 80cm long, 30cm wide and 30cm high.

5 Alpine trough An old sink is often recommended for an alpine container, but these are hard to come by nowadays. This concrete trough is 38cm long, 25cm wide and 13cm high – the smallest of several sizes available. The relatively wide surface is ideal for displaying a variety of small plants. As well as alpines such as dwarf phlox or saxifrage, it can be used for small bulbs or creeping herbs such as thymes. Alpines are shallow-rooting, so they suit shallow containers like this, although it is important to use a free-draining compost (mix one scoop of fine grit or perlite to four scoops of compost). Set off the planting with a thin mulch of fine gravel chippings.

6 Metal planter The hard-edged, industrial look of galvanized metal makes it a popular choice for contemporary patios, decks and roof gardens. Metal planters makes a wonderful setting for silver birches (*Betula pendula*), billowing grasses such as miscanthus or small leafy salads or herbs. The lightweight sheets of metal can be easily unbolted and stored flat, which is useful if you want to use the container for the summer months only and have limited storage space. When choosing metal containers, check how the edges and corners are finished; some are very sharp and could present a hazard. A range of sizes are available.

7 Corner planter This terracotta planter is designed to fit neatly into a corner. Semicircular planters that can be pushed right up against a wall are also available. Both make the best use of small spaces. When planting, position the largest plant in the centre, where there is plenty of room for the rootball to develop, and fill in the gaps with smaller temporary plants.

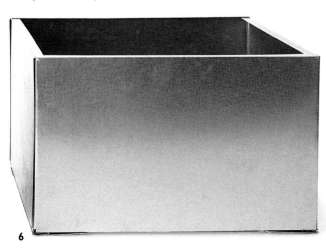

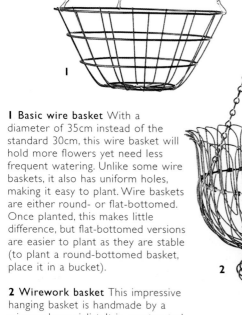

1 Basic wire basket With a diameter of 35cm instead of the standard 30cm, this wire basket will hold more flowers yet need less frequent watering. Unlike some wire baskets, it also has uniform holes, making it easy to plant. Wire baskets are either round- or flat-bottomed. Once planted, this makes little difference, but flat-bottomed versions are easier to plant as they are stable (to plant a round-bottomed basket, place it in a bucket).

2 Wirework basket This impressive hanging basket is handmade by a wirework specialist. It is constructed from galvanized steel finished in an antique patina. To show off the detail in this basket, line the sides and plant the top only with something special like scented violets.

3 Self-watering basket Hidden at the bottom of the basket is a water reservoir, which is topped up through a tube. Water passes from the reservoir up a wick to the compost. The solid sides of the basket make it quick to plant. Simply put a vigorous trailing plant such as a Surfinia-type petunia in the top, and it will grow down over the sides.

4 Wooden basket This teak basket is designed for orchids with aerial roots, although if lined, it can be used for other plants such as violets and foliage begonias. Orchids flower better when they are slightly pot-bound, so the idea is to keep the plant in the smaller container, which nestles inside the larger one, and the roots grow through the gaps between the slats.

hanging baskets

Hanging baskets offer one of the simplest ways to add summer colour. You do not even need a garden; just a sheltered spot where you can fix up a bracket. They also allow you to make the most of trailing plants such as pendulous begonias and helichrysums.

To create a ball of colour, you will need a wire basket so both the sides and the top can be planted; wire baskets need lining.

Hanging baskets require a certain amount of attention to look their best. In dry weather, they need watering daily. If this is not possible, use a bigger-than-average basket — a larger volume of compost will retain moisture for longer — or plant drought-tolerant species such as bidens, felicia or pelargoniums. Another solution is to use a self-watering basket.

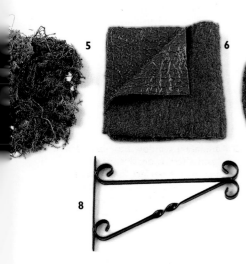

5 Moss The traditional lining for a wire basket, sphagnum moss is now in short supply in some regions. Like other loose lining materials, it has the advantage that it can be added to the basket a layer at a time while planting, which makes is easier to plant the sides fully, rather than having to cut holes in a liner. If moss is not available, experiment with natural substitutes like conifer clippings or even pieces of turf placed grass-side outwards.

6 Plastic-backed wool liner A variation on a pre-cut wool liner is this sheet of wool liner backed with perforated plastic that can be cut to size and used for wire baskets or troughs. The liner is laid in the basket with the wool side facing outwards. The plastic improves moisture retention.

7 Wool liner Wool is an effective substitute for moss and works well in winter baskets as it provides some insulation. A soft lining material, it is easier to cut or make holes in than stiff liners. Here the green wool has been made into a pre-cut liner; a brown version is also available.

8 Bracket A strong bracket securely fixed to the wall is needed to hold the weight of a hanging basket. This one is suitable for a 35cm diameter basket. When siting baskets, make sure they will not get in anyone's way, and avoid exposed sites.

window boxes

Window boxes enable you to grow flowers, herbs and some vegetables, even if you have no garden. They add a welcoming touch to the facade of your house and can also be used as troughs, laid alongside or even on top of flat walls, or hung from balconies.

Wood is the most versatile material for window boxes. It can be painted, stained or varnished to match the finish of your exterior woodwork, or decorated with stencilled patterns, shells or mosaics to create an individual feature. Liners made of plastic or recycled paper will not only protect the wood, but also allow you to quickly change a spring bedding scheme to a summer one. However, many wooden window boxes are too wide for the window ledges of modern houses.

Terracotta boxes share all the advantages of terracotta pots, and will fit in with most styles of architecture. However, the majority are relatively short. Metal window boxes offer an alternative look, and they work well with herbs. Many are equally at home indoors on the kitchen windowsill.

Plastic boxes are cheap and lightweight, so are useful if you want to use several to brighten up a balcony. There is a wide choice of sizes and colours, and if you need a drip tray, it is usually easy to get one to match. A drawback with cheaper plastic boxes is that they can soon bulge in the middle; some are sold with a thin plastic bridge to hold the sides straight.

When choosing a window box, consider how it will be fixed in place and measure the dimensions of the window ledge carefully. Take a tape measure with you when buying a box as not every measurement is always given. If you have a wide window ledge with sash windows or windows that open inwards, the box can be sited on the ledge. If your window ledge is too narrow for your chosen box, or if it slopes, the box can be attached to wooden or metal brackets set under the window. If the window opens outwards, choose low or trailing plants so it will not be obstructed.

1 Balcony bracket Cascades of red or pink geraniums draped over metal balconies are a characteristic of many European countries. The window box, let alone its supporting bracket, are rarely seen, but here is how such amazing effects are achieved. The metal bracket is hooked over the rail of the balcony, and the window box is attached to the bracket with metal clips.

2 Wooden window box Unlike many window boxes, this one comes ready-stained and with its own wooden brackets. It has short legs, so it can also be used on the ground as a trough. Belonging to a range that includes planters with a similar design, it can form part of a coordinated container display. The box is 85cm long, 25cm wide and 23cm high.

3 Terracotta window box The embossed fleur-de-lys pattern on this Italian window box gives it a classic look that would fit in well with a period house. This is an inexpensive terracotta box, and although not guaranteed frost proof, it is suitable for temporary plantings such as annual herbs, spring bulbs or small bedding plants.

4 Plastic window box Lightweight and inexpensive, this small, narrow window box is suitable for hanging from a balcony (using a balcony bracket) or for using as a liner inside a larger wooden or metal box. It is 45cm long, 16cm wide and 14cm high.

5 Aluminium window box Just 32cm long and 13cm wide, this metal window box is perfect for a kitchen windowsill, the top of a low wall or a garden table. Although small, it will hold three annual herbs or bedding plants. There are no drainage holes, so it is ideal for indoor use, as it will not drip. However, it is essential to add a layer of gravel for drainage.

specialist containers

Here is a selection of containers designed for specific types of plants. Aquatic planters control the spread of aquatic plants, many of which are very vigorous, while allowing their roots to push out through the mesh. Most are designed for placing on a marginal shelf at the edge of a pond, but lily baskets are often set on a pier of bricks in the centre. Aquatic baskets need a mulch of gravel to hold the compost in. Those with a wide mesh should be lined with hessian or garden fleece.

Strawberries and herbs can be grown in conventional containers, but the ones shown here take up very little space and are handy for positioning near the house.

1 Aquatic planters Available in a range of shapes and sizes, these mesh planters are ideal for controlling the growth of aquatics. Planters with a fine mesh, such as these, do not need lining. Use special aquatic compost or loam made from rotted turf; do not use soil containing organic matter as it will foul the water.

2 Flexible aquatic planter Flexible planters are made from a fabric called plantex, which is also used as a sheet mulch. They are surprisingly strong and take up less storage space than the plastic ones. They are worth considering if you keep fish as the soft edges will not cut them. Plastic planters can become brittle with age or split as the plants grow, which creates sharp edges. The flexible planter is available in two sizes: 18cm square and 25 x 25 x 20cm.

3 Water-lily basket A large basket is needed to contain water lilies, which are very vigorous, and this example is 45cm in diameter. A key feature to look for is handles on the sides, as these baskets are difficult to position in the water without them.

4 Strawberry pot Strawberry pots with holes in the sides hold the fruit away from the soil, thus ensuring it is the best quality; they also save space. With a diameter and height of about 40cm, this stoneware pot is a sensible size for a patio, and the hole at the top is large enough for you to reach right inside when planting and watering; many other pots are too small. The handles make it easier to move the container under cover to protect the fruit from birds without damaging the plants. The pot can also be used for herbs: try planting parsley or basil in the sides, with rosemary or sage in the top.

5 Bonsai pot To create a bonsai tree, the roots need to be restricted in a very small pot, while keeping the plant well watered and fed. This shallow glazed pot is typical of the containers used. Pots need to be frost-proof, as the plants are kept outside most of the time, and decorative.

6 Herb planter Herbs vary in their vigour, so they are best kept in separate containers. This ingenious planter has six sections, which fit together to make a hexagon. It is made of polypropylene and has plugs for blocking the drainage holes so the containers can be brought indoors without dripping. Use it for growing culinary herbs such as parsley, basil, chervil, sage, coriander and mint. Terracotta versions are available.

propagating plants

propagating pots and trays

A rewarding and cost-effective way of obtaining new plants for your garden is to propagate them yourself from seeds or cuttings. Most of the techniques are fairly straightforward and you'll need only a few items of equipment to get started.

The majority of seeds and some cuttings are started off in small pots or in trays under cover, and moved in stages to increasingly bigger containers before they are taken outside. In days gone by, gardeners used wooden trays and clay pots, but nowadays most people use plastic containers, which are lighter, cheaper and easier to clean. The combination of pots and trays that will best suit your needs depends on where the seeds or cuttings are to be raised – for example on

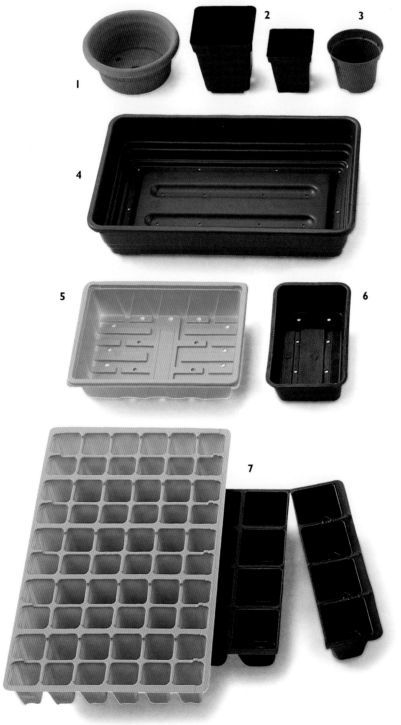

1 Terracotta seed pan Traditional terracotta seed pans like this one can still be purchased from potteries. Providing good aeration and drainage, they are ideal for seeds that are kept outdoors and that take a long time to germinate, such as the seeds of some trees and alpines.

2 Square plastic pots It is surprising that square pots are not more widely used as they are a more efficient use of space than round pots. A standard seed tray will take 15 of the small pots or 8 large ones.

3 Round plastic pot A typical plastic pot, with a diameter and depth of 8cm. Plastic pots are adequate for most seeds and cuttings. As well as being cheaper, they are also simpler to clean than terracotta pots, making it easier to provide the hygienic conditions required for propagation.

4 Seed tray This standard seed tray measures 38 x 24cm. It can be used to hold smaller trays, cellular inserts or a collection of small pots. Not only will it keep them tidy, but it prevents the pots being knocked over and makes it easier to move them around. Transparent covers with vents are available that will fit onto standard seed trays.

5 Half tray Two of these flexible plastic trays will fit inside a standard seed tray. This one is disposable, which saves on cleaning and storage.

6 Quarter tray Four of these will fit into a standard seed tray. This one is rigid so it is easy to wash and can be re-used many times.

7 Cellular inserts These thin plastic cellular inserts can be placed inside rigid trays. The black one has 24 cells and the green one 60 cells. When seedlings have three or four leaves, push each cell up from underneath and either plant out or pot up. Pushing out the rootball usually spoils the shape of the cell, so these types of inserts are used only once.

a windowsill or in a greenhouse – and the quantities involved. Standard seed trays are too large for most windowsills, and are useful only if you want to produce a large number of a few plants. If you simply want to grow a selection of half-hardy plants for filling the containers on a patio, a collection of half or quarter trays plus a dozen small pots gives more flexibility.

Another development, borrowed from commercial horticulture, is the cellular system, in which each plant has its own cell of compost. This makes for more uniform growth and reduces root damage at planting time. Cellular systems are most useful for annuals, where any root damage when planting out can lead to a check on growth from which the plant never recovers. Those with 24 cells per standard seed tray are ideal for most vegetables, but ones with 40–60 smaller cells per tray are a more efficient use of space for vegetables that can be transplanted when quite small, such as lettuce.

8 Peat pots Made of peat and wood pulp, these biodegradable pots can be planted in the ground along with the plant. They are therefore useful for plants that do not like to have their roots disturbed, such as most annual vegetables and bedding plants.

9 Grow tubes These bottomless grow tubes are designed for sowing seeds of plants with long tap roots such as sweet peas, beans and leeks. The pots are biodegradable, so they do not need to be removed before planting.

10 Root trainers The grooves in the side of these cells encourage a good root system to develop. A hinge allows you to open the cells and check the progress of the roots without having to remove the plants. This idea was developed for commercial growers, but this is a useful item for the keen amateur gardener who wants to propagate seeds or cuttings of plants that are difficult to root, such as deep-rooted trees and shrubs like eucalyptus, or seeds that remain in their pots for a long time, such as tree seeds. Unlike many modular systems, the plastic is thick enough to re-used.

11 Polystyrene cells Cellular trays made of polystyrene provide good insulation for roots, and if handled carefully, usually last for several seasons. The examples shown have 40 cells and will fit inside a standard seed tray. They often come with a 'multidibber', which is used with its pegs facing down to make holes for sowing, and then used with the pegs facing up to release the seedlings by pushing the base of the cells.

Growing from seed

Medium-sized seeds are fairly easy to sow. The seed is sown thinly in rows or scattered in pots or trays, and the resulting seedlings are then pricked out (spaced out into pots or cellular trays). A seed sower can be useful if your fingers are not very agile. A few plants, such as lobelia, begonia and impatiens, have seed so fine it is like dust. Mix these with some silver sand first to help you see where you have sown, and be prepared to prick out the seedlings more than once. Large seeds like nasturtiums and sunflowers are easy to handle – simply push one or two seeds into small pots or cellular trays of compost. The seeds can be spaced out so there is no need to thin seedlings later, although you could sow two seeds and remove the weaker seedling.

Sowing Use fresh multipurpose or seed and cutting compost. Break up any lumps with your fingers and fill the tray or pots to the brim. Firm gently with a tamper to give an even surface for sowing. Put the tray or pots in a shallow tray of water for a few minutes until the compost is moist. Sow the seed thinly to prevent overcrowding. After sowing, keep the seed in a warm place indoors or in a greenhouse, or stand it on a blanket propagator. Keep the compost moist by hand misting. Most annuals, perennials and vegetables germinate in one to three weeks.

Medium-sized seed Here medium-sized seed is sown with a seed sower to help space it out. After sowing, scatter a dusting of sieved compost over the seeds. To find the best spacing, you can experiment by 'sowing' the seed on paper with the sower at different settings.

Fine seed To sow fine seed, add silver sand to the packet, shake well, then tip the mixture onto a piece of folded paper. Sprinkle it on the compost. Many tiny seeds, such as impatiens, need light to germinate so leave them uncovered or sprinkle fine vermiculite over them.

Pricking out Once seedlings have their first pair of true leaves, they can be pricked out. Discard any weak or surplus seedlings and transplant the number of plants you require into pots. An exception to this is if you are sowing a mixture of plant colours that includes white. Usually, white-flowered varieties are weaker growing, so to get the full range of colours, you will need to keep some of the weaker seedlings as well.

1 Select the strongest-growing seedlings to prick out. Hold each one by one of its seed leaves and gently ease a dibber or widger under the plant to lift the roots. Transfer the seedling to a pot or cellular tray filled with compost.

2 Use a small dibber to make a hole and ease the seedling roots into it. Push the compost over the roots and firm in gently. The seedlings may look a bit floppy for a day or so. Return them to the propagator and allow them to recover for a few days.

1 Electric blanket Shaped to fit a greenhouse bench, an electric blanket provides a large heated area on which to stand an assortment of trays and pots. The blanket, which contains heated wire, is laid on polystyrene pads for insulation, and a sheet of polythene is laid over the blanket to protect it from water and soiling. Seed trays or pots are then placed on the polythene, and the bottom heat encourages seed germination or rooting. The temperature is controlled by a thermostat with an indicator light. When not in use, the blanket rolls up for easy storage.

2 Greenhouse propagator A typical-sized propagator for a greenhouse bench. A good feature of this one is the adjustable thermostat, which prevents overheating and allows you to fine tune the temperature to the type of seed or cuttings you want to propagate. Use it in conjunction with a thermometer for greater accuracy. The thermostat has an indicator light.

3 Windowsill propagator An ideal starter kit for sowing seed. The long narrow tray fits most windowsills, and comes with seven quarter trays with lids. This is a simple heated propagator that will keep the seeds 10–12° above room temperature, but there is no thermostat or indicator light, so you need to turn it off on warm days.

propagators

To achieve the highest rate of germination, most seeds need to be kept at a temperature of about 20°C. The easiest way to provide a controlled environment is to use a heated propagator. It can be sited in a heated greenhouse with an electricity supply or in a well-lit indoor location. A propagator can also be used for rooting cuttings.

A heated propagator consists of a plastic seed tray with a built-in heating element. This provides gentle warmth from the base and in most types is capable of raising the temperature of the compost up to 10°C above the room temperature. A transparent plastic top keeps the atmosphere moist, and adjustable ventilators can be used to increase or decrease the humidity.

The main drawback of a basic propagator is that the temperature inside is always about 10°C higher than it is outside, so you need to remember to turn it off on warm, sunny days or your seedlings will fry. A propagator with a built-in thermostat will turn itself off if it gets too hot – a feature that is well worth paying extra for. In the most sophisticated models, the maximum temperature can be adjusted to suit different types of seed.

Even the most powerful propagators will not be able to maintain 20°C if the surrounding temperature drops much below 5°C, so some background heating may be needed in a greenhouse or an unheated room indoors. Check the temperature inside a propagator with a maximum–minimum thermometer (see page 134).

If you want to use a windowsill propagator, the window should receive plenty of light, although young seedlings need to be shaded from direct sunlight, or they will be scorched. Seedlings will bend towards the light as they grow, so turn the pots daily to keep the stems growing straight.

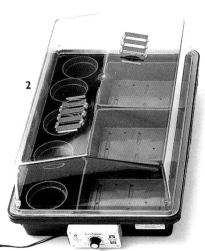

propagating paraphernalia

If you want to sow only a few seeds, you need very little in the way of equipment: a couple of pots and trays of compost and somewhere to keep them warm will suffice. The same applies to taking cuttings, although here you will also need a good knife or a scalpel (see page 70).

However, if you get hooked on propagating, it is worth buying a few extra items to speed up time-consuming processes such as preparing containers, sowing smaller seeds and pricking out seedlings. Small plant labels are useful if you want to sow a lot of seeds, as it is easy to forget what you have sown.

Most of the items featured here are small and easily mislaid, so it is a good idea to keep them all together, either on a shelf in a potting shed or in the corner of a potting tidy. The other useful pieces of equipment for propagating are hand misters (page 43) and thermometers (page 134).

1 Mini-cloches These plastic mini-cloches can be slipped over pots in seconds, avoiding the need to fiddle around with polythene bags held on with rubber bands. The two sizes shown fit pots with diameters of 13cm and 10cm.

2 Plastic labels Most plastic labels are white, but these are coloured, so are great for organizing plants ready for planting out. For example, you could use green ones for vegetables, orange for bedding plants, purple for perennials; or you could use different colours to distinguish between hardy and tender plants. Plastic labels are suitable for indoor use or for temporary use outside; after a year in the garden, they become brittle. Write the names with pencil, which is less likely to get washed off in a humid atmosphere, and you'll be able to re-use the labels.

3 Sieve A small plastic or metal sieve with a 3–12mm mesh will remove any lumps or fibres from the compost you scatter over your seeds after sowing and ensure they are evenly covered. Coir-based composts in particular often contain long fibres.

4 Plastic widger and dibber These tools are sold as a pair. The dibber makes holes for larger seeds or for cuttings (sowing depths are often given on the side). The widger is used later on for lifting seedlings or cuttings, and moving them on to the next size of container; either end of the widger can be used.

5 Steel widger Use this tool to lift seedlings or cuttings from small pots or trays to larger pots, with minimum root disturbance. It can be used either way up, depending on the size of the seedling or cutting.

6 Seed sower An inexpensive gadget that helps people with less agile fingers to sow seeds thinly. The seeds are placed in the circular container, the lid is adjusted to suit their size, and one seed is dispensed at a time. This device should cut down or eliminate the need to thin out seedlings.

Successful propagating

○ Always collect seed or take cuttings from healthy plants; water the plants well the day before taking cuttings.

○ Make sure pots are clean, and water seedlings and cuttings with tap water to avoid contamination.

○ Use a good-quality compost that can retain moisture without waterlogging; small pots and trays place great demands on a compost's ability to hold water. Seed or cutting composts are available, but a multipurpose one will do. The important thing is to start each season with a fresh bag.

○ Break up the compost with your fingers (it is often slightly compressed when you buy it) and overfill pots and trays, removing the excess with your hand. Press the compost down lightly with a tamper or with the base of another pot or tray. Firming down creates an even surface and ensures there will be good contact between the seeds or cuttings and the compost.

○ Sow thinly so there are spaces between each seed. Crowded seedlings are more likely to fail due to damping-off disease or simply because they are starved of light; they are also harder to prick out.

○ Seeds or cuttings need a transparent cover to create a humid atmosphere. A sheet of glass over a seed tray or a polythene bag over a pot are homemade solutions, but it is easier to use tailor-made covers.

7

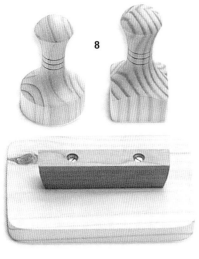

8

7 Potting tidy If you do not have a potting bench and are forced to fill your pots and trays with compost on the kitchen table, it is worth buying one of these inexpensive trays. It contains the compost in one place and provides you with a flat surface to work on. This one is ideal as it has high sides, feels stable and does not have any sharp edges. The holes in the handles can be used to hold dibbers, widgers and pencils for labelling.

8 Tampers These handmade wooden tampers are perfect for pressing the compost down gently prior to sowing seeds or inserting cuttings. There is a range of sizes and shapes to suit different containers; shown here are round and square ones for small pots and a rectangular one for a half tray. Tampers are sometimes known as 'presser boards'.

Taking cuttings

A knife is the ideal tool for propagation as it can cope with cuttings at different stages of ripeness. Secateurs can be used for hardwood cuttings, and a scalpel is useful for soft tissue such as leaves or softwood cuttings.

Hardwood cuttings This type of cutting is taken from shrubs and climbers in late autumn to midwinter after the current growth has matured, so use hand pruners to cut through the wood.

1 Cut the shoots into sections of equal length and thickness: a length of 20cm is typical for most plants. Here willow is being used; it can also be cut much longer if desired. To help you remember which way up to plant the cuttings, make a horizontal cut just below the node at the base of the shoot and a sloping cut away from a bud at the top.

2 Make a V-shaped trench with a spade and insert the cuttings, spacing them about 5cm apart with the sloping cut end uppermost. Firm the soil around the trench. Water the ground if it is dry, especially the following spring, and keep the area free of weeds. Lift the rooted plants in autumn and move them to their final site.

Leaf cuttings Some plants can produce roots and shoots from just a leaf or even a section of a leaf. Here the leaves of a *Begonia rex* are cut with a scalpel. Streptocarpus and gloxinias can be propagated in a similar way, but the cuts are made across the main vein. Leaf cuttings can be taken any time during the growing season.

1 Choose a large, healthy leaf from the parent plant. Cut away the stalk and lay the leaf down on a clean, flat surface with the leaf veins uppermost. Use a scalpel to cut out squares 2.5cm across, each with a main vein running through it.

2 With the veins facing downwards, pin the squares into a tray of free-draining compost. Keep the cuttings warm (21°C) and regularly moisten the compost with a hand mister until small plants develop. Separate the plantlets and pot them.

lawns and other surfaces

mowers

A healthy, well-maintained lawn is both a comfortable, practical surface and an attractive garden feature. The key to achieving a successful lawn is frequent mowing (at least once a week in the growing season) with a machine that will cope with its size and shape, and cut to the height required. If you have a lawn, a mower is one of the most important gardening tools you will need to buy. It may also be among your most expensive purchases, so careful selection is essential.

There are three basic types of mower: cylinder, rotary and hover. A rotary mower is one of the most flexible, as it cuts well at different grass heights, including longer grass. Those looking for a budget mower to quickly deal with a small family lawn will find hover mowers appealing, especially if the lawn is an awkward shape. If you want a neat, closely cropped lawn, a cylinder mower will give a crisp finish, although the best results are achieved with fine-leaved grasses. For a classic striped lawn, you will need a mower with a rear roller, which means choosing a cylinder type or some rotary models. To cope with rough grass, your best bet is a rotary mower with a high cutting height; it may be necessary to use a trimmer or scythe first.

When choosing a mower, note the cutting width of the blade, the grass-cutting height (and if it is adjustable), and whether there is a grass box. Check the handle is at a comfortable height. Mowers are hand driven or powered by a petrol engine, an electric motor or a motor with a rechargeable battery – the choice of power source comes down to size of lawn, budget and personal preference.

1 Cylinder hand mower A simple mower with a series of blades on a cylinder that rotate as the mower is pushed forwards to cut against a fixed blade. The blades are extremely sharp, producing a crisp, well-manicured finish. They should be used on grass that is kept short as they do not cope well with long grass. This mower has a detachable grass box. Hand mowers are quiet and economical to buy, run and maintain, and there is no electric cable to worry about. However, they are only practical for small, even lawns. Electric and petrol-driven cylinder mowers are available.

Mower speak

O **Cutting width** The wider the cutting width, the quicker you can cut an area of lawn, but the more difficult it is to cut around obstacles. As a guide, small mowers with a cutting width of 30cm are only feasible for lawns up to 100sq m. Mowers with a cutting width of 35–40cm can cope with lawns up to 250sq m. For a medium to large lawn, say 250–500sq m, a petrol mower with a cutting width of 42–50cm will save you time and effort. If you have a very large lawn (over 500sq m), consider a ride-on mower.

O **Cutting height** By adjusting the cutting height to suit the growth of the grass and the weather conditions, you can ensure the grass is not put under too much stress during dry spells or when making the first cut of the year. You may also want to adjust the cutting height to suit the style of different areas within the garden, or the way the lawn is used. For example, a family lawn needs to stand up to wear and tear, and letting it grow a little longer (about 2.5cm) will reduce stress on the grass. Although the cutting height can be adjusted on most mowers, some are easier to adjust than others and have more options – try adjusting the height in the shop before buying.

O **Grass collection** A grass box on a mower collects the clippings for composting, leaving the lawn neat and ready for use. However, the box adds to the weight, and some people prefer to mow without it, raking the clippings up afterwards or leaving them on the lawn. If the grass is cut little and often, the cuttings will decompose, but they may not do so if the weather turns cold. Some mowers have a mulching option – they can be set to shred the clippings finely and blow them back on the lawn. This feeds the lawn and protects it from drought. Some grass boxes are easier to remove and replace than others, and the size varies, so check them before buying.

2 Hover mower As the rotating blade cuts the grass, this mower hovers on a cushion of air, making it easy to manoeuvre around awkward shapes. The simplest models, such as the one shown here, are inexpensive, lightweight mowers with plastic blades, suitable for cutting small family lawns. The cutting height is adjustable. More expensive models have metal blades, which give a neater finish than plastic, and grass boxes.

3 Rechargeable mower Rechargeable mowers are growing in popularity as the running time of the batteries improves (typically 30–50 minutes on a single charge) and prices fall. They cut with a rotary action and are quieter to use than petrol machines, yet do not have the cable of electric mowers, so they score highly for convenience. This one has a grass box and the cutting height is adjustable.

4 Rotary mower Rotary mowers cut with a rotating metal blade. They can be powered by electric motors or by petrol engines, and although they are more expensive than basic electric hovers, they are more versatile. They usually have a grass box, and the cutting height can be adjusted to cope with short, medium and long grass. If you want a striped lawn, look for a model with a rear roller. If it is serviced regularly, a petrol rotary mower will last many years. The one shown has a grass box and a mulching option.

5 Ride-on mower A ride-on mower is an expensive item, but if you have a very large lawn, it will save you a considerable amount of time and effort. It is best to go to a specialist mower agent, armed with your lawn dimensions as well as the sizes of access points to the lawn and the storage area. The agent will advise on the most appropriate size for your needs and give you a demonstration or test drive. Check how comfortable the machine is and how easy to get on and off; how simple it is to control, especially when turning; how easy it is to tip or remove the grass box; and how versatile the mower is. Finally, ask about after-sales service. The model illustrated here has a 107cm cutting width, and is suitable for lawns up to 1.6 hectares. The lawn clippings can collected in twin bags, put through a mulching device to make them smaller or simply discharged as they are. Accessories are available for converting the mower into a tractor with a trailer or into a snow plough.

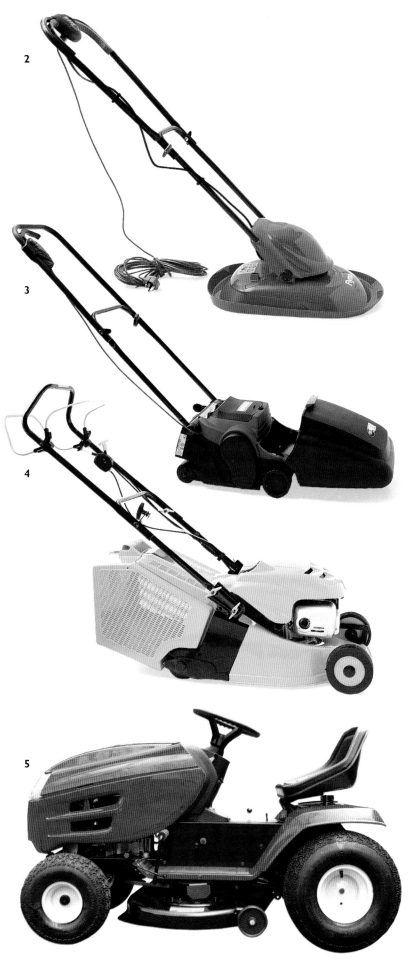

other grass-cutting tools

These are the tools for the grass-cutting tasks that a mower cannot cope with. Lawn shears are used to trim the edges of a conventional lawn. They have a scissor-like action, but the orientation of the blades varies. Particularly useful are those with vertical blades, which will trim grass growing sideways along borders and paths. Shears with horizontal blades are for cutting grass growing vertically in places a mower cannot reach, for example where a lawn meets a wall, or beneath trees and shrubs. If your garden has both types of lawn edge, look for a tool with blades whose orientation can be changed.

Powered trimmers can trim lawn edges quicker and with much less effort than lawn shears, but they do not produce such a neat finish. The cutting part of a powered trimmer is a nylon line that rotates very fast. The cheapest and most popular types are powered by mains electricity, but rechargeable, battery-operated ones are improving all the time, and because there is no electric cable, they are safer and easier to use. Petrol-powered trimmers (not illustrated) are heavy-duty tools capable of tackling woodier growth than long grass, but you need a fair amount of strength and the correct safety gear to handle one.

Trimmers have a protective cover to prevent stones and other debris from being spun out at the user, but it is still advisable to wear safety glasses and stout shoes as a precaution. Cut grass hitting the skin can cause 'trimmer rash', particularly on sunny days – if you have sensitive skin, cover your arms and legs and wear gloves.

Sickles and scythes are used for cutting meadow grass or hacking tall weeds, or for cutting grass where the ground is too rough or inaccessible for a mower. A sickle is used one-handed with a swinging action. Being shorter than a scythe, it is ideal for sloping ground or where there is not so much room to swing, for example to cut long grass growing between young shrubs or hedging. A scythe is a two-handed tool used with a twisting action. The shaft (or 'snath') was traditionally made of wood with two wooden handles, although aluminium is now often used. The blades are detachable, curved and of various lengths – there are left-handed blades available. Blades are usually carbon steel and need regular sharpening with a scythe stone.

To cut through turf, for example when repairing a lawn edge, laying turf or re-shaping a lawn, use a half-moon edger. Most have similar blades, typically 20cm wide and 10cm deep; some have a tread. The blade must be kept sharp. Buy a well-made edger with a secure socket that fits into the shaft. Handles have either a T or a D grip, and shafts are either wood, tubular steel or fibreglass.

1 Electric trimmer The least expensive power trimmer, an electric trimmer is lightweight to use and trims effectively. The model shown is one of the most basic, but it does have an automatic line feed, which is an important feature. As with any mains electric tool, always use it with RCD (residual current device) protection and an outdoor extension cable.

2 Rechargeable trimmer As it does not have a restrictive electric cable, a rechargeable trimmer can be used anywhere in the garden. This is a great advantage, particularly for dealing with long grass in a wildlife area at the bottom of the garden. Rechargeable trimmers cut for about 20 minutes on a single charge.

Choosing grass-cutting tools

When choosing any of these tools, hold them in the shop to check the weight and balance of the tool and the comfort of the handles. Tools with longer blades cut a bit quicker than those with shorter blades, but are not as precise for cutting around corners or curves. It is best to pick the tool you find less tiring, even if the job takes longer. Scissor-action tools should be opened and closed several times to check for a smooth action.

When buying a trimmer, hold it as you would if you were using it, to check that the handles are comfortable and the balance feels right. If you are tall, avoid models that require you to stoop to use them as this can lead to backache. If you are short, check that you can hold the trimmer comfortably without having to raise your arms and lift your shoulders into an unnatural position.

Most trimmers have adjustable heads that can be changed from a horizontal trimming mode to a vertical edging one. In use, the nylon cutting line breaks frequently, and more line needs to be fed from the spool. This is easy if the trimmer feeds out the line automatically but inconvenient if you have to stop trimming to do it manually.

3 Lawn shears These shears are used to trim the grass growing vertically at the edge of a lawn where it meets a wall or fence. They give a very neat finish, but can be tiring on the arms, so you need to be reasonably fit to use them, or have only a small lawn to trim. These have tubular steel handles to reduce the weight and chromed steel blades.

4 Edging shears The vertical blades of edging shears trim grass growing sideways, so are useful alongside borders or paths. They give a neat finish, but are not as quick as power trimmers. These have tubular metal handles with soft grips, and a non-stick coating that protects the blades against rust.

5 Multi shears The blades of multi shears can be rotated so both clipping and edging can be carried out with one tool. They have one long handle instead of two, which reduces the weight, but check that you can hold and operate them easily. Chromed steel blades reduce the risk of rust, and there is a safety catch.

6 Sickle A traditional tool for cutting rough grass and tough weeds. This one has a curved, flat, forged-steel blade that is ground on either side so it can be used by left- and right-handers. Sickle blades are about 40cm long, with wooden handles that are 13–15cm long.

7 Scythe This scythe has a traditional wooden snath, made of ash. The blades are purchased separately; the one shown here is 60cm long, but 75cm blades are available. The carbon-steel blade is pinned to a steel frame to help prevent the blade buckling or bending. There are two wooden handles, and their position can be adjusted to suit the user.

8 Half-moon edger As long as the blade edge is kept sharp, a half-moon edger cuts easily and cleanly through turf. This one has a carbon-steel head, so it is easy to sharpen. The shaft is made of wood and has a polypropylene D grip.

3 4 5 6 7 8

Using grass-cutting tools

1 Scythe Keeping your leading arm straight and your other arm slightly bent, hold the scythe at about a 45-degree angle to the ground and swing it by twisting your waist and hips, rather than your arms. Move the tool smoothly in a slow, arcing rhythm – do not hack at the grass. A scythe is most useful where there is plenty of room to swing it safely.

2 Sickle For cutting rough patches of weeds and grass in a small area, such as this uneven grassland with a young hazel coppice, a sickle is ideal as it is small enough to be used between other plants. Hold the sickle in one hand, grasp a handful of vegetation and swing the blade to cut underneath it. Because they are used one-handed and held close to the body, sickles are potentially more dangerous to the user than scythes.

3 Edging shears To keep a definite division between a lawn and a bed or border, trim the grass at the lawn edge with a tool designed for the purpose. Edging shears produce a particularly crisp finish. Standing on the lawn, hold the shears close to the edge and cut the grass, following the shape of the lawn.

Mowing a meadow

Michael Pollan is a celebrated American journalist and author of the award-winning book Second Nature, *an amusing and thought-provoking account of his ongoing tussle with nature in his New England garden (pictured opposite). In the book he asked 'Why mow?'. Here he relates what has happened since he decided to swap a mower for a scythe.*

'My meadow is essentially a half-acre of lapsed lawn: I simply stopped mowing the lawn to see what would happen, and what happens is meadow. Over the years, the community of plant species has changed, and I've found that by changing the time of year that I mow I can change the species. So, when I was getting far too much golden rod for my taste, I switched the mowing date from early autumn, which gave the golden rod time to set seed and spread, to midsummer, which cuts it down before it's had a chance to do any such thing.

I mow part of my meadow with a scythe I bought from Smith & Hawken, the mail-order garden tool company. It's a beauty – lightweight, with a long, yielding blade. The wood is ash, and everything about it is flexible enough to give when it encounters resistance. The blade collects nicks, bending rather than breaking (the whole concept is very Zen) when confronted with a rock or stump. This means you have to constantly maintain your blade, banging out the nicks and sharpening it with a stone, which is a perfectly pleasant occupation.

Once you get the rhythm, the swinging of the scythe feels as natural as breathing, and you can go forever. The sound of the blade cutting the grass is fine summer music, especially when you compare it to the roar of a mower. You cannot, however, cut a sharp, narrow path with a scythe (at least I can't) – and a sharply defined path is the key to a meadow looking like the product of human intent rather than neglect – so for that I resort to an old Toro mower.'

rakes, aerators and feeders

The tools featured here are used for raking up thatch (dead grass and moss) or leaves, applying fertilizers and aerating compacted ground. For a small lawn with no major problems, a spring-tine rake may be all you need, for raking up a few leaves and thatch. However, maintaining a large lawn or improving a problem lawn is much quicker and easier if you use the right equipment.

Anyone who has to deal with falling leaves in autumn will need at least one leaf rake and perhaps another sweeping or collecting tool (see page 128). Other specialized rakes are used for raking meadows, sand, gravel and other hard surfaces. For a leaf-collecting rake, the choice of material comes down to personal preference – do you prefer a precision-made metal tool or a rustic one? Do you want to use it on other surfaces? Will a noisy rake bother you? The best rake for removing thatch is a metal spring-tine rake. The wider the rake head, the quicker it will cover the ground, but if your lawn

1 Spring-tine rake A springy wire rake is ideal for removing thatch from a small lawn. In this one, the ends of the steel tines point down at an angle that ensures good contact with the ground. With a head width of 43cm, it can double as a small leaf rake.

2 Detachable scarifier rake The teeth of this rake dig deep into the lawn on the pull stroke to remove thatch. An effective tool, it is worth considering if you have a serious thatch problem, but use it with care or you could pull up living grass. The 30cm head snaps onto a handle of your choice. For details of interchangeable systems, see page 9.

3 Rubber rake This tool comes with two rubber heads: a 38cm-wide rake head and a 30cm-wide broom head. With its flexible tines, the rake will sweep small amounts of leaves and grass clippings from lawns and other surfaces without digging into the ground or making a noise. The broom can be used wet or dry to sweep or scrub. The telescopic metal handle extends to 135cm.

4 Small detachable rake A rake with a narrow head for collecting leaves and grass clippings from narrow spaces or hard-to-reach areas, such as under hedges. The lightweight head is made from reinforced polymer. It can be attached to a short handle for close work or a long one for inaccessible areas. For details of interchangeable systems, see page 9.

5 Detachable plastic rake The flat tines of this rake are designed for gently combing the lawn to remove grass clippings or fallen leaves. Being plastic, it is lightweight and easy to use. The head is 43cm wide, which means it can gather a large pile of debris quickly. A 130cm handle is recommended. For details of interchangeable systems, see page 9.

6 Self-cleaning rake This leaf and grass rake has back supports that allow debris to build up on the rake. When the rake is full, it is turned to allow the debris to fall into a wheelbarrow or bag. At 63cm wide, the rake head can cope with a large lawn. The head and teeth are made of polypropylene and the handle is wood.

7 Bamboo rake These rakes are imported from China and sold in the autumn for leaf clearing. They are cheap and lightweight, but the tines are not evenly spaced or aligned. They last several years before the ends wear out or become too uneven to use. To prevent the tines drying out, wash in water at the start of autumn. The rake head is 45cm wide.

8 Sand rake The symbolic patterns raked in sand or gravel in Japanese gardens are created with special rakes that are handmade by the gardeners. This one is made of ash and was obtained from a bonsai nursery. It is similar to a hay rake, but the narrower head (43cm) is easier to hold steady, and the teeth are wedge-shaped at the ends to make furrows.

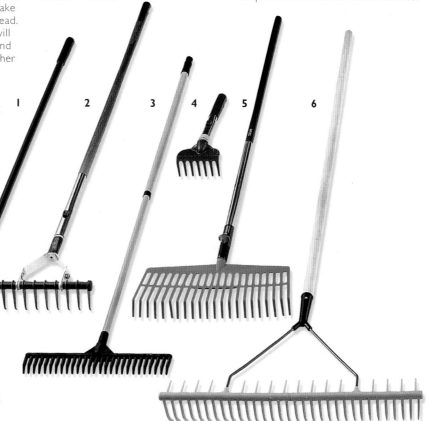

is small or has a complex shape, do not buy one that is too wide. For a serious thatch problem, use a scarifier rake or an electric rake.

In areas of lawn subjected to heavy use, the ground can become compacted, making re-seeding difficult. Aerating compacted areas every year or two will improve the chances of grass re-establishing. The soil can be spiked with a garden fork, but a specialized tool takes out cores of earth so a lawn topdressing can be swept in, which will greatly improve the soil.

Lawn fertilizers should be applied evenly to avoid a patchy effect. Many fertilizers come with applicators, but for small lawns, it can be cheaper to buy a hand dispenser. For a medium-sized or large lawn, it is worth getting a wheeled spreader.

9 Hay rake A traditional rake for gathering hay from a wildflower meadow. The 76cm-wide head makes for quick raking. Being all wood, it is lightweight and easy to handle; the curved section helps to support the large head. It can also double as a levelling rake for smoothing topsoil before laying a lawn.

10 Detachable hollow-tine aerator This tool takes the hard work out of aerating a compacted lawn. It is pressed into the ground to make two holes, up to 6cm deep, into which sand or lawn topdressing can be brushed. The head is 22cm wide, and the tines are replaceable. A T-shaped handle is recommended. For details of interchangeable systems, see page 9.

11 Electric lawn rake An electric rake has teeth on a rotating roller. It takes the effort out of thatch removal and is worth considering for larger lawns, where using a spring-tine rake would be time-consuming and tiring. This one has a collecting box, which saves having to rake up the thatch.

12 Hand-held spreader This is a convenient dispenser for spreading grass seed or lawn fertilizer evenly over a small- to medium-sized lawn. It holds 1kg of fertilizer, which will cover an area measuring 7 x 7m. There are five settings to cover different types of seeds, and a range of fertilizer application rates. Hold the full dispenser on one arm with your hand on the trigger; use your other hand to turn the handle as you walk across the lawn.

13 Wheeled rotary spreader A wheeled spreader is pushed along the lawn, and a hopper dispenses the correct amount of fertilizer granules or powder. Machines are usually pre-set to take particular brands of fertilizer, but it is possible to re-set them for other brands. This spreader has a rotary action so the fertilizer is dispensed over a larger area than a simple drop spreader.

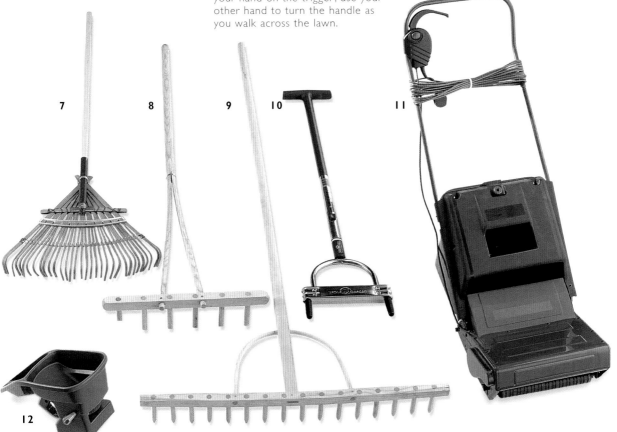

Using lawn-care tools

1 Spring-tine rake Hold the rake with your thumbs pointing upwards on the shaft and scratch up the dead grass and moss from the soil surface. If you have a severe moss problem, apply mosskiller a few weeks beforehand and rake off the dead moss; raking live moss can spread the problem. This type of raking is called scarifying. It is hard work, but it improves the health of the grass, and any feed applied will go right down into the soil. Scarifying is best done in spring or autumn.

2 Aerator Heavy wear on a lawn not only damages the growth of the grass, but compacts the ground underneath, making it difficult for the grass roots to penetrate the soil. By removing cores of earth, an aerator opens up the ground and improves drainage. It also enables you to brush in soil improvers. Aerate when the soil is moist – autumn or spring are good times – and avoid extremes such as droughts, wet weather or frosts. Work across the lawn to remove the cores evenly. Sweep them up and brush in a topdressing to improve the soil.

3 Fertilizer spreader Yellow-green lawns benefit from feeding as the growing season gets underway. The light colour is caused by a lack of nitrogen in the soil; in this case, it was leached away from the sandy soil by heavy winter rains. For a small or medium-sized lawn, a hand spreader is adequate.

Raking sand or gravel in a Japanese garden

Marc Peter Keane is a leading authority on Japanese garden design, and lectures on the subject at Kyoto University of Arts and Design. A successful author and landscape architect, he has designed many Japanese gardens, including the Spiral Garden in Kyoto, shown opposite. Here he explains how to create a sand or gravel garden.

'The Japanese have a long tradition of raking sand or gravel into symbolic patterns, a tradition I have followed in my own work. In the Spiral Garden, the crisp lines in the sand act as a counterpoint to the hills of moss, creating a balance between the 'designed beauty' of human culture and the 'organic beauty' of wild nature.

To create a sand or gravel garden, lay a 3–5cm-deep layer of sand or gravel straight onto compacted earth. A layer of concrete under the gravel is sometimes recommended, but this creates a hot feel to the feature. I wouldn't advocate using sheet mulch, either – if it's not buried deeply enough, the teeth of the rake catch in the fabric; if it's too deep, it won't work. Authentic sand is composed of quartz, feldspar and mica, which gives a salt and pepper effect. Use whatever material is local to your area; small gravel 5–10mm in diameter is a good size for raking.

In Japan, the rakes are handmade by the gardeners, using branches from conifers. There are two styles of rake: one has dowels inserted into a piece of wood to make a rake head; the other has a wooden board cut at one end to form a zigzag. A big flat bar is used to flatten the sand or gravel, then a rake is used while walking backwards, half bent over, to make the lines. I suggest starting with simple straight lines. Once you have mastered these, practice patterns. The idea is you should be calm and at peace while you rake; if you hurry or are stressed, the lines will be wiggly. When priests in Zen temples rake, it is not done as a chore but as part of their meditation.'

sweepers and blowers

A leaf rake is more than adequate for sweeping up fallen leaves in small areas, but if you are faced with the annual headache of large quantities of leaves and other debris falling over extensive areas, one or more of the following tools will be invaluable.

Which tools to choose depends on the type and size of surface, and whether you prefer using simple hand tools or powered equipment. If you have a rotary mower with a grass box, an alternative solution is to set the mower to its highest setting and collect the leaves in the box.

It is vital to remove leaves from areas where they might cause accidents – wet leaves on steps or paths, for example. Leaves on lawns and low-growing plants like alpines and herbs should also be cleared – not only do they look messy, if the leaves become wet or diseased, they will weaken the plants and spread diseases. Leaves that fall on the ground in beds and borders can be left to rot down and enrich the soil, as they would in natural woodland. To prevent leaves polluting water in the garden, cover ponds with netting before leaf fall (see page 88), and make sure gutters and water barrels do not become clogged up.

1 Besom For tasks like sweeping leaves and other debris, simple rustic items like this compete well with more sophisticated tools. The springiness in the twigs gently flicks leaves and wormcasts off lawns without damaging the grass. These items have a limited life, but are inexpensive and can be recycled by simply adding the twigs to the compost heap. Smaller versions are sold as witches brooms around Halloween, so you might get the children to sweep the leaves for you.

2 Grabber hands A simple product that is fun to use and surprisingly effective. Slip your hands into the straps, and you have giant grabber hands that can scoop up and lift piles of leaves. The grabbers featured here are comfortable and easy to use; those with handles at the top of giant hands can be awkward to manoeuvre.

3 Stiff broom A stiff broom is efficient at removing wet leaves from paved areas and decking, as the bristles scrape off the slimy residue from decomposing leaves as well as the leaves themselves. The one featured is a patio broom, which is easier to use in small areas and on steps. A yard broom is a more heavy-duty tool, useful for larger areas.

4 Powered leaf blower and vac Powered tools come into their own for blowing leaves and hedge trimmings off areas that rakes and brooms cannot reach, such as borders. As well as vacuuming the leaves into a bag, this machine will shred them as well, which reduces their bulk and means that more can be collected before the bag needs emptying.

carrying and storing

equipment for carrying

Gardening involves carrying items of all shapes and sizes, from bags of topsoil to hedge trimmings, from shrubs that need transplanting to harvested fruit and vegetables. Using the right equipment to move things around makes a lot of difference to the speed and effectiveness of many gardening tasks, as well as your enjoyment of them.

When choosing equipment for carrying, make sure it is suitable for the size and the topography of your garden, as well as what you plan to grow in it. While a wheelbarrow may be essential if you want to grow your own produce or renovate a large garden, it might not be of much use if you have a steeply sloping plot or a tiny backyard. Write a list of all the carrying tasks in your garden and note any problems of access or movement. This will help you to choose the equipment that will best meet your needs.

For transporting bulky, heavy loads such as soil, hardcore, gravel, manure and compost, containers need to be strong, durable, easy to move and easy to load and unload. For most situations, a wheelbarrow is the best option. To get the most from a wheelbarrow, the garden needs to be accessible via paths or other hard-landscaped areas, although as a temporary measure you can lay planks over bare earth, steps and even lawns. When buying a wheelbarrow, try it out for ease of steering around corners and tipping out. A garden wheelbarrow is lighter and easier to move than a builder's barrow, although the latter copes better with heavy-duty items such as hard landscaping materials. Wheelbarrows come with either a solid or a pneumatic tyre; the latter are easier to manoeuvre, but are prone to puncturing on thorns or stones as they are usually only 2- or 4-ply. A good tip is to get a tyre dealer to fit a 6-ply trailer tyre onto your wheelbarrow as the thicker tread will make it more durable.

For moving bulky, light loads such as grass clippings, fallen leaves, hedge trimmings, dead top growth from deadheading or cutting down perennials and some mulches such as bark chips, containers need to hold a high volume of material yet be light. They should be easy to fill, carry or drag along, and tip out. Large bags and carrying sheets are ideal for these tasks.

Containers for carrying harvested produce such as cut flowers, and crops ranging from root vegetables and tree fruit to leafy herbs, vegetables and soft fruit, need to keep the produce in good condition. They should allow crops to be laid flat without too much being piled on top. A container that can be held in one hand while harvesting, such as a flower basket or trug, is ideal. To prevent crushing, carry tree fruits and root crops separately from soft fruits and leafy herbs and vegetables.

I

I Wheelbarrow This example of a good garden wheelbarrow is lightweight and easy to handle, yet surprisingly strong, able to cope with heavy materials such as hardcore as well as lighter items. The lightness and strength reside in the polypropylene tray, which will not rust, and the wheel has bearings, so it moves smoothly. The tip bar in front of the wheel makes it easy to tip the contents out of the barrow.

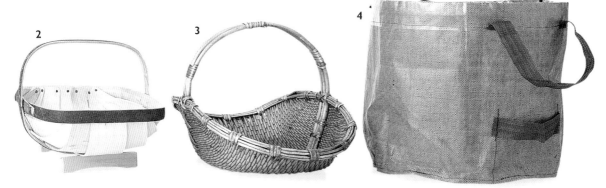

2 Trug Light, strong and appealing, the traditional English trug is still popular all over the world for carrying harvested crops and cut flowers. Nowadays, most trugs are mass-produced, but this is the real thing, made by craftsmen from coppiced wood. The darker wood used for the handle and frame is split chestnut and the lighter boards

are willow, all held together with copper nails. Trugs come in different sizes (the larger ones were once used as a measure of volume); this is a small garden trug – a number 6, measuring 50 × 28cm.

3 Flower basket Cheaper and lighter than a trug, this cane basket is fine for holding flowers cut from the garden, harvesting soft fruit or

collecting material after deadheading. The flat bottom and open sides are ideal for keeping cut flowers in tip-top condition.

4 Large bag Use bags such as this to carry or drag light but bulky debris like leaves and hedge clippings. They are much better than bin liners as the bag stays open by itself, so you can use both hands to feed in material. This one comes flat packed and is held open by a strip of plastic fed through the rim, which can be removed for storage.

Buckets
For a cheap, sturdy and versatile carrier, a bucket is hard to beat. Buckets will hold both solids and liquids, and the carrying handle means you can have one in each hand for balanced load carrying, or hook one over your arm while harvesting. Also use them for mixing composts, scooping out debris from ponds, or if they are clean and dry, for storing other tools.

5 The galvanized metal bucket is a classic design that fits into any garden style. Eventually the seams or the bottom will go, resulting in the so-called 'bottomless bucket,' which can be used to contain mint growing in the garden.

6 The plastic bucket is lighter and quieter than the galvanized bucket, but is just as tough. The plastic roller grip on the handle makes it more comfortable to hold when transporting heavy loads.

7 A recent development in bucket design is the tubtrug. Made from recycled rubber, it can do everything a bucket can do, and its flexibility makes it easy to carry and pour from.

8 Carrying sheet Also known as a tarpaulin sheet, this is useful when several people are working on a big project, such as pruning a shrub border or trimming a hedge. Lightweight material is dumped on the sheet, which is then dragged along using the handles at the corners. Woven polypropylene is the ideal material as it is light but strong, and does not rot or stain.

storage equipment

Most fruit and vegetables are best eaten fresh, but a few crops can be stored through the winter. Potatoes, apples and pears need a dark, dry, cool but frost-free (above 4°C) place like a cellar, shed or garage. Other vegetables such as onions, garlic, marrows, pumpkins, winter squash and winter cabbage need similar conditions, but can be stored in the light. Tender ornamental bulbs, corms and tubers can be kept year after year if lifted, dried and stored in a cool but dry frost-free place.

When putting crops and bulbs into cool storage, use trays and boxes that allow air to circulate through the produce, such as ones made of slatted wood or plastic mesh, or bags with a loose weave or mesh. Fruits keep longer if they are wrapped individually in parchment paper. Most seed packets contain more seed than you need in a season; store the surplus in an airtight container in a refrigerator.

Storage sense

O Store only healthy bulbs and tubers; discard any that show signs of disease, such as softening of the tissue, or that have been damaged.
O Dry bulbs and tubers overnight; as a precaution against storage rots, you can dust them with fungicide.
O Rub off soil and any loose tissue or dying foliage from potatoes, onion and garlic before storing to reduce the likelihood of rot.
O Check stored produce regularly and remove any rotting fruit or vegetables promptly.
O Store different varieties of crops or bulbs separately and label them.
O Protect the store from rats and mice.

1 Hessian sacks Tightly woven yet permeable, these sacks are ideal for storing potatoes in the dark. The larger ones shown here are hessian sacks; the smaller ones are hessian sandbags, which can be hung on pegs or beams. Double-thickness paper sacks are an alternative for storing potatoes, but not plastic bags as they create a humid atmosphere. Take care not to overfill the sacks, and tie them securely at the necks.

2 Mesh bags Use mesh bags with drawstrings to store onions, garlic, winter cabbage or bulbs. The drawstring can be used to hang them up and so save space.

3 Wooden seed trays Traditional seed trays are ideal for storing ornamental bulbs and tubers over winter, or for keeping small quantities of apples, wrapped in greaseproof paper.

4 Apple crate For storing large quantities of apples, use an apple crate, but wrap each fruit separately in greaseproof paper. A solid wooden box (i.e. one that is not slatted) can be filled with moist sand and used to store root crops such as carrots.

5 Plastic stacking trays These versatile trays can be used on their own or stacked to make a storage unit for vegetables, fruit such as pears, and bulbs. With mesh bottoms that allow good air circulation, they are also good for drying onions, garlic or bulbs before storing.

6 Seed storage box Once seed packets have been opened, any surplus seed must be stored in an airtight container to maintain seed viability. This food storage container is a good size for seed packets, and being transparent, it is easy to identify the contents.

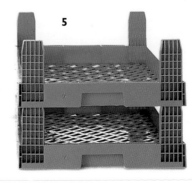

planning

measuring and marking

Most gardening tasks require very little equipment for precise measuring and marking out. However, there are occasions when precision at an early stage can yield much better results. For example, measuring the acidity of your soil will indicate which plants are suited to it and which are not. Poor seed germination is usually a result of sowing too early before the soil or compost is warm enough – let a thermometer rather than the calendar be your guide when sowing.

Garden design and construction tasks such as building a patio involve marking out and measuring the site to estimate quantities of materials and to ensure accurate construction: the area may also need to be levelled. Such projects require the use of basic DIY tools such as a spirit level and a builder's square, as well as landscaping equipment like a garden line and datum pegs.

When choosing measuring equipment, check that it will give the level of accuracy you need for a given task, and that any graduations can be seen clearly. And read carefully any instructions explaining how equipment should be positioned and maintained.

Using a thermometer A thermometer measures the air or soil temperature around it (or its probe), so place it exactly where you want to take the measurement. In a greenhouse, for example, it should be placed among the plants rather than up against the glass. When propagating seeds, you need to measure the temperature of the soil or compost rather than the air, so push the base of the thermometer down to the depth you want to sow. Protect a thermometer from direct sunlight and draughts, for example by making a simple wooden stand.

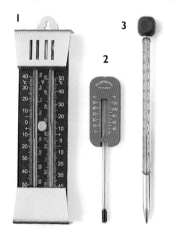

1 Maximum–minimum thermometer This thermometer will show the current, maximum and minimum temperatures since it was last set. You can use this information to check if the heating in a greenhouse or conservatory is working at night or if there is overheating during the day. The minimum night-time temperature is often the critical factor in deciding what tender plants to grow.

2 Compost thermometer
An inexpensive thermometer for checking the compost temperature when germinating seeds or rooting cuttings. This will be more accurate than relying on the thermostat on a propagator.

3 Soil thermometer Improve the germination rate of outdoor sowings by using a soil thermometer to judge the ideal sowing time. It has a metal tip so it can be pushed into the soil to the same depth as the seed drill. Take the temperature every morning until it shows for several days the minimum temperature needed to sow any given seed.

4 Digital thermometer
This battery-operated thermometer gives the current, maximum and minimum temperatures in digital form, which is clearer and easier to read than calibrations up the side. You can set the display to read in either Celsius or Fahrenheit, and the numbers are very clear, even from some distance. Attached to the display unit is a 3m flex with a remote sensor at the end. This enables you to either fix the display to a wall or move it around as necessary so it can be seen without compromising the location of the sensor.

5 Rain gauge Measuring the rainfall in your garden will indicate if you need to set up an irrigation system or water some areas more than others. To compare your records with official ones, an open position where there is no rain shadow is best. To see how much rain reaches a bed by the house or how long to leave the sprinkler on, site the gauge in the area you want to know about. This one has a spike that is inserted into the ground; others are designed for mounting on a post (30cm high is ideal). Keep daily records and remember to empty the gauge after each reading.

6 Compost scoop In planting or propagating recipes, bulk ingredients for making compost are usually specified as parts by volume. For example, a seed compost might be two parts loam, one part peat and one part sand. A simple scoop such as this is useful for measuring out the bulky ingredients in such recipes or to make up your own.

7 Soil testing kit This simple, inexpensive kit is a useful first step in assessing the chemical nature of your soil – information that is invaluable when choosing plants. It comprises four containers, for testing pH and the major plant nutrients: nitrogen, phosphorus and potassium. Particularly useful is the pH test, which will give you an instant indication of whether your soil is acid or alkaline just by comparing the colour of the solution with the colour chart supplied.

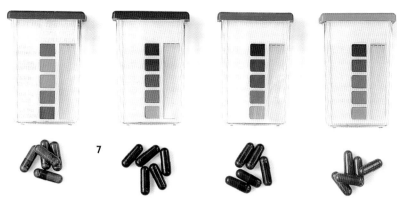

7

8 Spirit level When laying a lawn or hard landscaping materials such as brickwork, or erecting fence posts, check the level with a spirit level. This one has a digital display and can be set to beep, which is more accurate than looking at a bubble, particularly when you are working in confined spaces or on a muddy site.

9 Builder's square A formal garden design comprising straight paths and square or rectangular features such as lawns, beds and ponds needs to be marked out precisely on the ground if it is to look professional. Used in conjunction with a garden line, a builder's square will enable you to ensure that the corners of such features are truly at 90 degrees.

10 Tape measure This 8m measure is a handy pocket size, and can be used for measuring features in the garden and when shopping for items like containers. To measure a whole garden for a survey, a 30m measure is easier to use; these can be hired from DIY hire shops.

11 Datum pegs Made by cutting hardwood stakes to identical lengths, datum pegs are used with a spirit level for checking the level over a large area, such as when laying a lawn or patio. Draw a mark on each peg at the same distance from the top. Knock a grid of pegs in the ground so the marks are the height of the level you want. Use a spirit level to check the pegs are the same height, then rake the soil to the level marked on the stakes.

12 Marker paint A quick way to mark out informal shapes in a garden is to use an aerosol can of marker paint. It can be sprayed on asphalt, gravel, concrete or grass, and dries in about 30 minutes. This 750ml can is enough for a run of about 100m, assuming a line 5cm wide.

Garden lines These are used to mark straight lines for design or planting projects such as building a wall, putting in a run of hedging, sowing vegetables or planting bulbs in long rows. Most garden lines have two pointed stakes, one of which holds a reel containing the line. Shown here is a handcrafted wooden example (**13**) and a classic metal one (**14**). Both are substantial, which is an advantage as the smaller ones with plastic stakes tend to get lost.

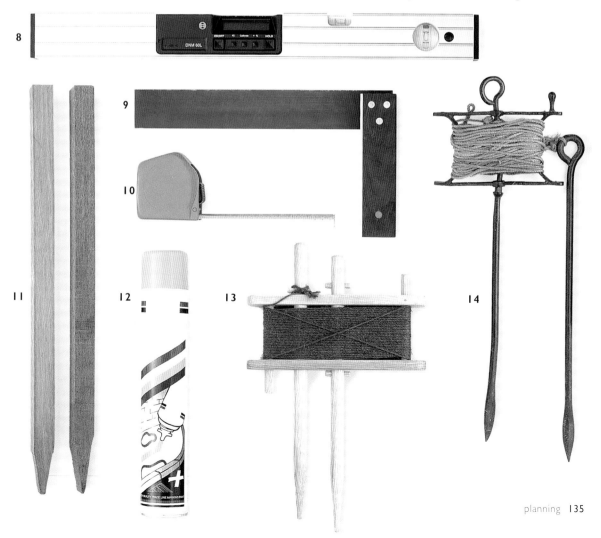

Testing the soil

Soil is tested in test tubes, so the samples are only a tiny proportion of the total area of soil you need to know about. For this reason, it is vital to obtain a sample that is representative of the whole area. Large areas are best divided into sections that are tested individually, particularly if the garden has many levels.

A simple and inexpensive pH testing kit will give you a rough idea of what your soil is like – whether it is acid, neutral or alkaline. For a detailed analysis of the nutrients present, you will need to send the samples to a soil laboratory.

Soil tests should be carried out before adding any fertilizers, chemical weedkillers, pesticides or mulches.

1 Lay out 4 bamboo canes in a W shape across the area to be tested. Smaller areas, say between two shrubs, can be tested by laying two canes in an X shape and taking the samples at the end of each cane and in the centre where the canes cross.

2 Use a clean trowel to take out some soil at each of the 5 points at the ends of the canes. Dig down to about 10–15cm. Remove any stones and bits of root and crush any lumps of soil. Mix the five soil portions together in a clean bucket and take out the amount needed for the test (usually 500g for a full laboratory analysis).

3 To test the soil pH yourself, using a testing kit, take a half teaspoon of the soil and drop it into the test tube of chemical supplied. Add water and shake well. Check the colour of the resulting liquid against the colour chart supplied.

Using the results Knowing whether your soil is acid or alkaline can help you choose the right trees and shrubs for your garden, as many are acid lovers that will struggle on an alkaline soil. A neutral soil has a pH of 7, but most garden plants, including most fruits and lawn grass mixtures, prefer a slightly acid soil with a pH of 6–6.5. Acid-loving plants like azaleas, camellias and some heathers prefer a soil with a pH of 4–6. Soils above pH7 are alkaline, and plants that thrive in such soils are called lime-lovers.

There is little point in trying to make an alkaline soil more acid – a much easier option is to grow acid-loving plants in containers filled with lime-free (ericaceous) compost. Acid soils can be made more alkaline by adding lime (in the form of ground limestone). This is worth doing if you want to grow vegetables, as most like a pH of 6.5–7.5; brassicas prefer the upper part of this range.

gardening gear

protective equipment

Gardening is a physical activity that involves working in all weathers and handling a wide range of materials, plants and equipment, some of which are potentially hazardous. Although they appear at the end of the book, the items featured here are extremely important, as they help to make gardening tasks safer, easier and more comfortable.

Gloves are invaluable, and it is worth having a couple of pairs for different jobs and weather conditions, say a lightweight pair that keeps your hands clean but allows you to use your fingers easily and a sturdier pair to protect your hands from grazes or thorns. Always try on gloves to check the fit as the sizes can vary greatly. Check how well your wrists are protected, and look for loose stitching and snags. With leather gloves, there may be a natural variability in the quality of different pairs.

As when buying other footwear, try on shoes and boots before buying, preferably with the socks you are planning to wear with them. Gardening footwear needs to be comfortable, waterproof and robust enough for the task (boots for digging should give the soles adequate protection).

1 Woolly gloves Just the thing to wear for winter pruning. The mitten part peels back to reveal fingerless gloves that keep your hands warm, but allow your fingers to handle pruning tools with ease.

2 Leather and suede gauntlets These heavy-duty gloves offer protection when handling sharp-edged landscaping materials, prevent splinters when working with rough timber, and guard against prickles when pruning thorny shrubs. The protective leather covers the hand, and the suede extends over the wrist.

3 Nitrile-coated cotton gloves These gloves combine the comfortable, cooling feel of cotton with the strength of nitrile (a type of PVC), which protects the fingers from thorns and sharp objects. They are good gloves to wear when pruning roses.

4 Rubber gloves A heavy-duty version of washing-up gloves, these are ideal for handling chemicals, cleaning a greenhouse or tending to aquatic plants. Rubber gloves with a cotton lining are more comfortable in warm weather. Longer versions are available for cleaning out ponds.

5 Disposable gloves A pack of disposable gloves is invaluable for all sorts of uses around the garden and the home. Being disposable, they are ideal for people who lose their gloves frequently or forget to store them correctly. They keep your hands clean and dry, yet are thin enough for you to undertake tasks such as planting, removing diseased plant material or cleaning containers with dexterity. Note that although they are waterproof, these gloves are open at the wrist, so they should not be used for handling concentrated chemicals.

6 Kneeler Kneeling in the garden is much more bearable if you have something to cushion and protect your knees and your clothes. This inexpensive foam pad is easy to use and store. It will not last long if left outside, so remember to clean it after use and keep it indoors.

7 Kneeling stool This kneeler helps you to get up after kneeling; just push on the struts at the sides. Turn it the other way up, and it becomes a garden stool. It is large enough not to lose in the garden, which often happens with the smaller kneeler pads. The only drawback is that it is tricky to assemble.

8 Kneepads Once you get used to wearing them, these strap-on kneepads are ideal if you need to move around a lot while working, for example, to weed or plant a large area like a vegetable plot or a new border. These pads are more comfortable than most as they are cushioned and shaped to fit the knee.

6

7

8

9 Ear defenders When using noisy power tools, such as petrol hedgetrimmers and some shredders, protect your ears from damage with ear defenders. Store them in a dry place and check the cushions periodically for wear and tear.

10 Goggles Wear goggles to protect your eyes when using power tools such as shredders, trimmers and hedgetrimmers, or when carrying out building tasks such as cutting paving slabs with a chisel or angle grinder. Handle and store them carefully as scratches will impair visibility.

11 Hat This waterproof hat is the ideal shape to wear when gardening. The rim is large enough to keep the rain out of your face without impeding visibility. The hat also rolls up easily for slipping in your pocket. A similar shape in cotton would be suitable for the warmer months.

12 Tool belt A tool belt will hold your secateurs, garden knife and some plant ties, so you can keep the few items you need for standing tasks, such as training wall shrubs and climbers or deadheading plants in hanging baskets, close to hand, without having to bend down. This one is made of durable lightweight nylon with strong nylon webbing for the edging and straps. The open mesh of the pockets helps to filter out sand and soil.

13 Clogs Until someone invents waterproof slippers, these smart gardening clogs are just the thing for slipping on to potter about on the patio or lawn, or to do the evening watering in the greenhouse. They are made of PVC and have cushioned soles and grip treads. Although handy for watering, they should not be worn when digging, mowing or carrying heavy items, or when working up a ladder.

14 Wellington boots Wellingtons are essential wear when gardening in wet and muddy conditions. These boots were originally designed to cope with Scotland's rugged terrain in unpredictable weather. They are made of natural rubber, and the sole is cushioned against impact. Variations on basic wellington boots include those with steel toe caps for protecting toes while moving heavy items and extra-long boots (waders) for venturing into ponds.

15 Walking boots It is a well-kept secret among professional gardeners that good-quality walking or hiking boots with leather uppers and rubber soles make ideal footwear for gardening. They keep your feet warm, dry and well protected, and the thick soles cope superbly with the rigours of digging.

sources

The following list will help you track down specific items featured in this book. Wherever possible, we have given manufacturers so you can contact them to find stockists in your area (see Manufacturers and Distributors, page 141). If the manufacturers are unknown, we have given retail outlets from which the items can be bought (see page 142 for contact details). Tool names used by manufacturers and the ranges or systems to which tools belong are given in brackets.

Page

8 wire brush by Harris; secateur sharpener by Felco; file by Chillington

12–13 1 traditional spade (Heritage range), 2 stainless-steel spade (Neverbend range) by Spear & Jackson; 3 traditional long-handled spade by Bulldog; 4 modern long-handled spade (power spade) by Wilkinson Sword; 5 draining spade by Sneeboer & ZN; 6 the bigfoot from Draper Tools

14 1 border fork, 2 stainless-steel garden fork by Yeoman; 3 manure or dung fork by Sneeboer & ZN; 4 potato fork by Bulldog; 5 spork from Dr Growgood

15 1 round-point shovel by Spear & Jackson; 2 square-point shovel by Bulldog; 3 mattock-pick head and handle from Knights; 4 heavy-duty hoe by Chillington; 5 duck-foot digger by Burgon & Ball

18–19 1 basic garden rake by Yeoman; 2 detachable bow rake (Multichange system) by Wolf Garden; 3 landscaping rake (landscraper) by Chelwood; 4 add-on handles by Peta; 5 hand rake by Sneeboer & ZN; 6 detachable flower rake (Combisystem) by Gardena; 7 detachable three-pronged cultivator (Multichange system) by Wolf Garden; 8 three-pronged cultivator by Wilkinson Sword; 9 detachable four-star tiller (Combisystem) by Gardena; 10 manure drag by Bulldog; 11 Canterbury fork by Chillington

22–23 1 basic draw hoe by Wilkinson Sword; 2 detachable draw hoe (Multichange system) by Wolf Garden; 3 three-pronged hand hoe by V&B Groundbreakers; 4 detachable two-pronged hand hoe (Combisystem) by Gardena; 5 onion hoe by Sorby Hutton; 6 angle weeder by Sneeboer & ZN; 7 ridging hoe by Chillington; 8 warren hoe by Bulldog; 9 Dutch hoe by Yeoman; 10 swoe by Wilkinson Sword; 11 winged weeder by Burgon & Ball; 12 oscillating hoe from Suffolk Herbs; 13 circlehoe by Henningsen

26–27 1 taproot weeder (daisy weeder) by Sneeboer & ZN; 2 weeding fork (Jekyll weeder) by Hortus Ornamenti; 3 hand fork (Neverbend range) by Spear & Jackson; 4 long-handled hand fork by Wilkinson Sword; 5 paving weeder by Yeoman; 6 weeding knife by Wolf Garden; 7 pointing trowel by RST, from Fairalls; 8 ibis from Organic Gardening Catalogue; 9 core weeder (miracle weeder) by Wilkinson Sword; 10 spot weeder by Weedeezy; 11 pond net by Laguna; 12 pond weeder (easy weeder) by Oasis

30–31 1 modern border spade (Neverbend range) by Spear & Jackson; 2 traditional border spade by Bulldog; 3 planting spade (universal planter) by Le Prince Jardinier; 4 long-handled trowel by Sorby Hutton; 5 standard-width trowel by CK; 6 narrow-width trowel by Yeoman; 7 right-angled trowel (planter hand) from Suffolk Herbs; 8 Peta fist-grip trowel by Peta

34–35 1 short-handled bulb planter by Bahco; 2 quick-release bulb planter by Gardena; 3 long-handled bulb planter by Yeoman; 4 metal-tipped wooden dibber, 5 large wooden dibber from Knights; 6 L-shaped plastic dibber by Tenax rapitest; 7 straight metal dibber from author's collection; 8 Wood and bamboo labels by Andrew Crace, 9 copper label with tie by Hallmark; other copper labels, 10 aluminium labels (alitags), 11 punching kit by Andrew Crace

42–43 1 traditional metal watering can from Baileys Home and Garden; 2 metal long-reach watering can, 3 plastic long-reach plastic watering can, 4 indoor watering can, 5 brass rose, 6 hand mister by Haws; 7 pressure sprayer, 8 pressure sprayer with lance by Hozelock; 9 knapsack sprayer by Di Martino

46–47 1 green hose by Hozelock, yellow hose by Rehau; 2 curly hose and lance from Agriframes; 3 wall guide by Hozelock; 4 spiked hose guide by Rehau; 5 brass connector by Rehau; 6 double check valve, 7 plastic connector by Hozelock; 8 repair connector, 9 stop connector by Gardena; 10 4-way connector, 11 simple water timer by Hozelock; 12 advanced water timer, 13 portable hose trolley by Gardena; 14 wall-mounted reel by Hozelock

48 1 sprinkler hose by Rehau; 2 seep hose by Leakypipe; 3 drip irrigation by Gardena; 4 gravity-fed system by Harcoster

50–51 1 spray nozzle by Gardena; 2 adjustable spray gun by Rehau; 3 rose-head spray gun by Hozelock; 4 feeder by Scotts; 5 lance by Gardena; 6 rotating sprinkler by Rehau; 7 static sprinkler by Gardena; 8 oscillating sprinkler, 9 pulse-jet sprinkler by Hozelock; 10 mobile sprinkler (rain train) by LR Nelson Co., from LBS; 11 ornamental sprinkler from Waterdance Creations

52 1 round water barrel, 2 stand by Harcoster; 3 wall-mounted water butt from Agriframes; 4 rain diverter by Plantpak; 5 capillary matting from Two Wests & Elliott

53 1 plastic compost bin by Tenax rapitest; 2 wormery by Can-o-Worms; 3 sieve by Sankey; 4 wooden compost bin from Agriframes; 5 shredder (quiet shredder) by Atco-Qualcast.

56–57 1 anvil secateurs by Gardena; 2 bypass hand secateurs, 3 holster by Felco; 4 gear secateurs by Wilkinson Sword; 5 ratchet secateurs by CK; 6 comfort-fit secateurs by Wolf Garden; 7 by-pass loppers by Yeoman; 8 gear-action loppers by Wilkinson Sword; 9 ratchet loppers by CK; 10 pole pruner (universal cutter) by Wilkinson Sword

60 1 folding pruning saw by Corona; 2 pruning saw, 3 scabbard by ARS, from Suffolk Herbs; 4 bow saw by Bahco; 5 rootcutter by Sharksaw; 6 saw attachment for pole pruner (universal cutter) by Wilkinson Sword

62–63 1 notched shears by Wilkinson Sword; 2 gear-action shears by Gardena; 3 telescopic shears (Razorsharp range) by Spear & Jackson; 4 trimming shears, 5 topiary shears by Burgon & Ball; 6 swivel shears by Wolf Garden; 7 electric hedgetrimmer by Black & Decker; 8 rechargeable hedgetrimmer by Ryobi

70–71 1 grafting knife by Tina; 2 budding knife by Victorinox; 3 scalpel by Swann-Morton; 4 harvest knife by Hand Tools; 5 pruning knife by Opinel; 6 asparagus knife by Arabella Lennox Boyd; 7 billhook by Burgon & Ball; 8 household scissors by Wilkinson Sword; 9 floral clip (Razorsharp range) by Spear & Jackson; 10 thinning shears by Corona; 11 ikebana shears by Zwilling JA Henckels; 12 cut-and-hold scissors by Victorinox

74–75 1 container obelisk (florabelle) from Agriframes; 2 bamboo obelisk by Andrew Crace; 3 metal obelisk by Shore Hall Garden Designs; 4 wooden obelisk by Plane and Simple; 5 metal trellis by Metal Art Works; 6 wooden trellis by Stuart Garden Architecture; 7 globe and spiral by Burgon & Ball; 8 elephant by Andrew Crace

77 1 pea sticks, 2 hazel poles from Traditional Woodland Services; 3 tree stake from Wyevale; 4 bamboo canes, 5 metal rods by Bosmere; 6 terracotta finial from Two Wests & Elliott; 7 split canes by Bosmere; 8 cane caps by Chandra Crafts, 9 plastic cane grip by Tenax rapitest; 10 metal coil by Bosmere

78 1 stiff netting by Tenax rapitest, 2 flexible netting from Homebase; 3 wire, 4 tension bolts from Knights; 5 wall fixings from Arabella Lennox Boyd; 6 loop stakes, 7 link stakes by Link Stakes; 8 ring stake by GroThru

79 1 raffia by Netlon; 2 natural string from Jacqueline Edge; 3 polypropylene twine by Tenax rapitest; 4 Velcro ties by Velcro; 5 chainlink strap (locktie tree strapping), 6 tree tie with buckle, 7 supersoft tree tie, 8 rose tie, 9 plastic ties from J Toms; 10 plant rings by Tenax rapitest

82–83 1 cold frame by Larch Lap; 2 square lantern cloche from Pevex Enterprises; 3 round lantern cloche by Arabella Lennox Boyd; 4 forcing pot by Whichford Pottery; 5 row cloche (longrow cloche) from Consumer Direct; 6 bell jar (solar bells) by Haxnicks; 7 polycarbonate cloche from Agriframes

86 1 sheet mulch, 2 black polythene from J Toms; 3 clear polythene from Tenax rapitest; 4 bubble insulation from Netlon; 5 hessian from Wolfin Textiles; 6 white fleece, 7 green fleece by Agralan; 8 dot-matrix shading from Two Wests & Elliott; 9 knitted polyethylene from Homebase 10 pegs by Agralan

88 1 wire netting from Homebase; 2 pond netting by Tenax rapitest; 3 fine mesh (enviromesh) by Agralan; 4 fruit netting by Netlon; 5 bark wrap (spiral guard), 6 stem guard (strimmer guard), 7 shrub shelter (correx shrubmaster) from J Toms; 8 bamboo dome from Andrew Crace, willow dome by The Old Basket Supply Ltd

90–91 1 terracotta flowerpots, 2 terracotta long tom, 3 shallow terracotta pot by Whichford Pottery; 4 plastic pot from author's collection; 5 terrazzo pot by CH Brannam; 6 glazed pots by Apta; 7 metal pot from author's collection; 8 glazed wall pot by Apta; 9 wicker wall pot by Growing Success; 10 plastic wall pot by Sankey

92–93 1 plastic tub by Stewart; 2 glazed ceramic pot by Eschbach, from Knights; 3 large terracotta pot by Whichford Pottery; 4 fibreglass pot, 5 fibreglass urn and pedestal by Capital Garden Products; 6 cast-stone bowl and urn by Cranborne Stone; 7 angle-top pot by Apta

96–97 1 Versailles planter by Designs in Wood; 2 fibreglass planter by Capital Garden Products; 3 wooden trough by Hillhout; 4 plastic trough by Stewart; 5 alpine trough by Sherston Earl, from Knights; 6 metal planter from www.dig-it.co.uk; 7 corner planter by Apta

98 1 basic wire basket by Fyba; 2 wirework basket by Rayment; 3 self-watering basket by Ward; 4 wooden basket (orchid box) from Jacqueline Edge; 5 natural moss from Bosmere; 6 plastic-backed wool liner by Supamoss; 7 wool liner, 8 bracket by Fyba

99 1 balcony bracket by Jardifer, from Knights; 2 wooden window box by ADK Marketing; 3 terracotta window box from Knights; 4 plastic window box by Sankey; 5 aluminium window box from Judy Green

104 1 aquatic planters by Hozelock; 2 flexible aquatic planter (aquaplanter) by Tetra; 3 water-lily basket from Bradshaws; 4 strawberry pot from Errington Reay; 5 bonsai pot by Tongrae Pots, from Wyevale; 6 herb planter by Netlon

106–107 1 terracotta seed pan by Whichford Pottery, 2 square plastic pots by LBS, 3 round plastic pot by Ward; 4 seed tray by Stewart; 5 half tray by Plantpak; 6 quarter tray by Ward; 7 black cellular insert from LBS, green cellular insert by Plantpak; 8 peat pots, 9 grow tubes by Fyba; 10 root trainers by Haxnicks; 11 polystyrene cells by Parasene

109 1 electric blanket by Two Wests & Elliott; 2 greenhouse propagator by Sankey; 3 windowsill propagator by Garland.

110–111 1 mini-cloches by Haxnicks; 2 plastic labels from LBS; 3 sieve, 4 plastic widger and dibber; 5 steel widger by Netlon; 6 seed sower by Tenax rapitest; 7 potting tidy by Sankey; 8 tampers by Chandra Crafts

114–115 1 cylinder hand mower by Al-Ko; 2 hover mower by Flymo; 3 rechargeable mower by Atco-Qualcast; 4 rotary mower by Al-Ko; 5 ride-on mower by Lawnflite

116–117 1 electric trimmer by Flymo; 2 rechargeable trimmer by Black & Decker; 3 lawn shears by Wilkinson Sword; 4 edging shears by CK; 5 multi shears by Wilkinson Sword; 6 sickle, 7 scythe, 8 half-moon edger by Bulldog

124–125 1 spring-tine rake by First Choice Ambassador; 2 detachable scarifier rake (Multichange system) by Wolf Garden; 3 rubber rake from author's collection; 4 small detachable rake (Multichange system) by Wolf Garden; 5 detachable rake (Combisystem) by Gardena; 6 self-cleaning rake by Chelwood; 7 bamboo rake from Knights; 8 sand rake from Japanese Garden & Bonsai Nursery; 9 hay rake by Bulldog; 10 detachable hollow-tine aerator (Multichange system) by Wolf Garden; 11 electric lawn rake by Atco-Qualcast; 12 hand-held spreader, 13 wheeled rotary spreader by Scotts

128 1 besom from Knights; 2 grabber hands by Tenax rapitest; 3 stiff broom (patio broom) by Salmon Products; 4 powered leaf blower and vac (mastervac) by Black & Decker

130–131 1 wheelbarrow by Fort; 2 trug by The Truggery; 3 flower basket from Knights; 4 large bag by Bosmere; 5 galvanized metal bucket, 6 plastic bucket from Fairalls; 7 Tubtrug by Faulks & Co.; 6 carrying sheet by Bosmere

132 1 hessian sacks from Baileys Home and Garden, 2 mesh bags from LBS; 3 wooden seed trays, 4 apple crate from Baileys Home and Garden; 5 plastic stacking trays from LBS; 6 seed storage box from author's collection.

134–135 1 maximum-minimum thermometer by West Meters; 2 compost thermometer by Brannan; 3 soil thermometer by West Meters; 4 digital thermometer by Diplex; 5 rain gauge, 6 compost scoop by Bosmere; 7 soil-testing kit by Tenax rapitest; 8 spirit level by Bosch; 9 builder's square by CK; 10 tape measure by Fairalls; 11 datum pegs by Nortene; 12 marker paint by Sealocrete; 13 wooden garden line from The Truggery, metal garden line from Baileys Home and Garden

138–139 1 woolly gloves, 2 leather and suede gauntlets, 3 nitrile-coated cotton gloves, 4 rubber gloves, 5 disposable gloves by Town & Country; 6 kneeler by Bosmere; 7 kneeling stool by Hozelock; 8 knee pads by Town & Country; 9 ear defenders from author's collection; 10 goggles by Martcare, from LBS; 11 hat by Stormfit; 12 tool belt, 13 clogs by Town & Country; 14 wellington boots by Gates; 15 walking boots by Scarpa

manufacturers and distributors

Use this list with the Sources list on page 140 to track down items featured in this book. Contact manufacturers or distributors for details of your nearest stockist or for a mail-order supplier. Some manufacturers such as potteries and woodworkers both make and sell to the public; full addresses for these are given under the Retailers list on page 142. If there is no UK manufacturer or distributor we have given the address of the main office abroad.

ADK Marketing 1 Lincoln Road, Leasingham, Sleaford, Lincolnshire NG34 8JS Tel 01529 304926
ARS UK distributor: Burton McCall Ltd – see entry.
Agralan Ltd See under Mail Order Companies, page 142.
Al-Ko Kober Ltd South Warwickshire Business Park, Kineton Road, Southam, Warwickshire CV47 0AL Tel 01926 818500 www.al-ko.co.uk
Andrew Crace See under Mail Order Companies, page 142.
Apta Pottery Dencora Way, Leacon Road, Fairwood Business Park, Ashford, Kent TN23 4FH Tel 01233 621090 www.apta.co.uk
Arabella Lennox Boyd Garden Products Ltd See under Mail Order Companies, page 142.
Atco-Qualcast Suffolk Works, Stowmarket, Suffolk IP14 1EY Tel 01449 742130 www.qualcast.co.uk
Bahco Tools Ltd Manor Way, Halesowen, West Midlands B62 8QZ Tel 0121 504 5220
Black & Decker Ltd 210 Bath Road, Slough, Berkshire SL1 3YD Tel 01753 511234 www.blackanddecker.com
Bosch Lawn and Garden Suffolk Works, Stowmarket, Suffolk IP14 1EY Tel 01449 742220 www.bosch-pt.de
Bosmere Products Ltd Unit 5, Mitchell Way, Airport Service Road, Portsmouth, Hampshire PO3 5PR Tel 02392 639890 www.bosmere.com
CH Brannam Ltd See under Mail Order Companies, page 142.
S Brannan & Sons Ltd Leconfield Industrial Estate, Cleator Moor, Cumbria CA25 5QE Tel 01946 816600 www.brannan.co.uk
Bulldog Record Bulldog Tools Ltd, Parkway Works, Sheffield S9 3BL Tel 0114 251 9190
Burgon & Ball Ltd La Plata Works, Holme Lane, Sheffield S6 4JY Tel 0114 233 8262
Burton McCall Ltd 163 Parker Drive, Leicester, LE4 0JP Tel 0116 234 4646 www.burton-mccall.co.uk
CK CeKa Works Ltd, Pwllheli, Gwynedd, North Wales LL53 5LH Tel 01758 701070 www.ck-tools.com
Capital Garden Products Ltd Gibbs Reed Barn, Pashley Road, Ticehurst, East Sussex TN5 7HE Tel 01580 202092
Chandra Crafts See under Mail Order Companies, page 142.
Chelwood Tool Co. See under Mail Order Companies, page 142.
Chillington The Chillington Tool Co., Crocodile House, Strawberry Lane, Willenhall, West Midlands WV13 3RS Tel 01902 826826 www.Chillington.co.uk
Consumer Direct See under Mail Order Companies, page 142.
Corona UK distributor: PLM Power Products, Units 5 & 6, Shires Industrial Estate, Essington Close, Birmingham Road, Lichfield, Staffffordshire WS14 9AZ Tel 01543 414477
Cranborne Stone See under Mail Order Companies, page 142.
Designs in Wood See under Mail Order Companies, page 142.
Di Martino UK distributor: Willowdale Products Ltd, Three Bridge Mill, Twyford, Buckinghamshire MK18 4DY Tel 01296 733922
Diplex Ltd See under Mail Order Companies, page 142.
Draper Tools Draper Tools Ltd, Hursley Road, Chandler's Ford, Eastleigh, Hampshire SO53 1YF Tel 023 8049 4333 www.draper.co.uk
Faulks & Co. 1 Frisby Court, Slingsby Close, Nuneaton CV11 6RP Tel 024 7638 8600 www.faulks.co.uk
Felco UK distributor: Burton McCall Ltd – see entry.
First Choice, Ambassador Spread Garden Supplies, Edward Street, St Helens, Merseyside WA9 3DS Tel 01744 753431.
Flymo Outdoor Products Preston Road, Aycliffe Industrial Estate, Newton Aycliffe, County Durham DL5 6UP Tel 01325 300303 www.flymo.com
Fort Wheelbarrows Ltd PO Box 330, Woking, Surrey GU22 9XS Tel 01483 727898
The Fyba Pot Co. Malvern Road, Knottingley, West Yorkshire WF11 8EG Tel 01977 677676 www.william-sinclair.co.uk

Gardena UK 27–28 Blezard Business Park, Brankley Way, Seaton Burn, Newcastle-upon-Tyne NE13 6DS Tel 0191 217 1537 www.gardena.co.uk
Garland Products Ltd First Avenue, The Pensnett Estate, Kingswingford, West Midlands DY6 7TZ Tel 01384 278256 www.garlandproducts.com
The Gates Rubber Co. Ltd Edinburgh Road, Dumfries DG1 1QA, Scotland Tel 01387 269591 www.gates-rubber.com
Gro Thru Plant Supports 792 Weston Road, Slough, Berkshire SL1 4HR Tel 01753 521992
Growing Success Wessex Horticultural Products Group, 1–3 Hilltop Business Park, Devizes Road, Salisbury, Wiltshire SP3 4UF Tel 01722 337744 www.wessexhort.co.uk
Hallmark Identification Products See under Mail Order Companies, page 142.
Hand Tools Co. See The Standard Manufacturing Co.
Harcoster Garden Products Windover Rd, Huntingdon, Cambridgeshire PE29 7EE Tel 01480 445114 www.harcoster.co.uk
Haws Watering Cans 120 Beakes Road, Smethwick, West Midlands B67 5AB Tel 0121 420 2494 www.haws.co.uk
Haxnicks Ltd See under Mail Order Companies, page 142.
Henningsen Index innovations Inc., 50 Sparkes Road, Sebastopol, CA 95472, USA For UK garden centre stockists contact infor@circlehoe.com
Hillhout Ltd Unit 18, Ellough Industrial Estate, Ellough Road, Beccles, Suffolk NR34 7TD Tel 01502 718091 www.hillhout.com
Hortus Ornamenti See under Mail Order Companies, page 142.
Hozelock Ltd Haddenham, Aylesbury, Bucks HP17 8JD Tel 01844 292002 www.hozelock.com
Japanese Garden & Bonsai Nursery St Mawgan Village, Cornwall TR8 4ET Tel 01637 860116
Laguna Rolf C Hagan UK Ltd, California Drive, Whitwood Industrial Estate, Castleford, West Yorks WF10 5QH Tel 01977 556622 www.hagen.com
Larch Lap Ltd Unit 291 & 296 Hartlebury Trading Estate, Crown Lane, Hartlebury, Worcestershire, DY10 4JB Tel 01299 251175
Lawnflite EP Barrus Ltd, Launton Road, Bicester, Oxon OX6 0UR Tel 01869 363636 www.barrus.co.uk
Leakypipe See under Mail Order Companies, page 142.
Le Prince Jardinier UK agent: Catriona McLean, Sanquhar House, Sanquhar, Dumfriesshire DG4 6JL. Scotland Tel 01659 50399
LG Harris & Co. Ltd Stoke Prior, Bromsgrove, Worcestershire B60 4AE Tel 01527 575441 www.lgharris.co.uk
Link-Stakes See under Mail Order Companies, page 142.
Martcare Worsham Mill, Minster Lovell, Oxford OX8 5RX Tel 01993 824000
Metal Art Works See under Mail Order Companies, page 142.
Netlon Sentinel Apollo House, Neepsend Lane, Sheffield, South Yorkshire S3 8AU Tel 0114 221 3401
Nortene Ltd Linehall House, Stanley Street, Chester CH1 2LR Tel 01244 346193 www.nortene.com
Oasis Water Garden Products Oasis House, Deer Park Industrial Estate, Knowle Lane, Fair Oak, Eastleigh, Hampshire SO50 7PZ Tel 023 8060 2602
The Old Basket Supply Ltd Unit 20, Hedges and Butler Site, Sugar House Lane, London E15 2QS Tel 020 8221 9700
Opinel UK distributor: Whitby & Company, Aynam Mills, Canal Head North, Kendal, Cumbria LA9 7BY Tel 01539 721032
Parasene Metpost Ltd, Mardy Road, Cardiff CF3 2EX, Wales Tel 029 2077 7877 www.metpost.com
Peta UK Ltd Mark's Hall, Mark's Hall Lane, Maragret Roding, Chelmsford, Essex CM6 1QT Tel 01245 231811 www.peta-uk.com
Plane & Simple See under Mail Order Companies, page 142.
Plantpak Synprodo Plantpak Ltd, Burnham Road, Mundon, Maldon, Essex CM9 6NT Tel 01621 745500
Rayment See under Mail Order Companies, page 142.
Rehau Ltd Hill Court, Walford, Ross-on-Wye, Herefordshire, RH9 5QN Tel 01989 762600 www.rehau.co.uk
Ryobi Power Equipment UK Ltd Pavilion 1, Olympus Park Business Centre, Quedgeley, Gloucestershire GL2 4NF Tel 01452 7274777
Salmon Products The Hill Brush Co. Ltd, Woodlands Road, Mere, Wiltshire BA12 6BS Tel 01747 860494 www.hillbrush.com
Sankey Richard Sankey & Son Ltd, Bennerley Road, Bulwell, Nottingham NG6 8PE Tel 0115 927 7335 www.rsankey.co.uk
SCARPA Mountain Boot Co. Ltd, Head Office, 8 Nelson St, Newcastle-upon-Tyne NE1 5AW Tel 0191 296 0212 www.scarpa.co.uk

The Scotts Company UK Ltd Salisbury House, Catteshall Lane, Godalming, Surrey GU7 1XE Tel 01483 410210
Sealocrete PLA Ltd Greenfield Lane, Rochdale OL11 2LD Tel 01706 352255
Sharksaw UK distributor: Oakthrift plc, Unit 7, Mill Hill Industrial Estate, Flower Lane, London NW7 2HU Tel 020 8906 2255
Sherston Earl Unit 5, Babdown Airfield, Tetbury, Gloucestershire GL8 8YL Tel 01666 505551 www.sherston-earl.co.uk
Shore Hall Garden Designs See under Mail Order Companies, page 142.
Sneeboer & ZN UK distributor: Link-Stakes Ltd, Upper Boddington, Daventry, Northamptonshire NN11 6DH Tel 01327 260329
Sorby Hutton See The Standard Manufacturing Co.
Spear & Jackson Atlas Way, Atlas North, Sheffield, North Yorkshire S4 7QQ Tel 0114 281 4242 www.spear-and-jackson.co.uk
The Standard Manufacturing Co. 55 Woods Lane, Derby DE22 3UD Tel 01332 343369
Stewart Group Holdings Waddon Marsh Way, Purley Way, Croydon CR9 4HS Tel 020 8686 2231
Stormfit Leisure Unit 1 Church Farm, Church Road, Barrow, Bury St Edmunds, Suffolk IP29 5AX Tel 01284 811365
Stuart Garden Architecture See under Mail Order Companies, page 142.
Supamoss UK Ltd 14 St Paul's Place, Halliwell, Bolton, Lancashire BL1 8BR Tel 01204 494221
Swann-Morton Ltd Oulerton Green, Sheffield, South Yorkshire S6 2BJ Tel 0114 234 4231 www.swann-morton.com
Tenax rapitest Tenax UK Ltd, Unit 12, Ash Road, Wrexham Industrial Estate, Wrexham LL13 9JT Tel 01978 664667 www.tenax.net
Tetra UK Mitchell House, 40–60 Southampton Road, Eastleigh, Hampshire SO50 9XD Tel 01703 628865 www.tetra-fish.com
Tina UK distributor: Burton McCall Ltd – see entry.
Tongrae Pots Kyoto Bonsai, Pinfold House, Crown Lane, Lower Peover, Knutsford, Cheshire WA16 9QA Tel 01565 723759
Town & Country Whitwick Business Park, Stenson Road, Whitwick, Leicestershire LE67 4JP Tel 01530 830990 www.townandco.com
The Truggery See under Mail Order Companies, page 142.
V&B Groundbreakers UK distributor: Chesterman Marketing Ltd, 3 Kenworthy Road, Astonfields Industrial Estate, Stafford ST16 3DY Tel 01785 250341
Velcro Ltd 1 Aston Way, Middlewich, Cheshire CW10 0HS Tel 01606 738806
Victorinox UK distributor: Burton McCall Ltd – see entry.
Ward Plysu Brands Ltd, Wolseley Road, Woburn Road Industrial Estate, Kempston, Bedford MK42 7UD Tel 01234 841771 www.wardproducts.co.uk
WaterDance Creations See under Mail Order Companies, page 142.
Weedeezy UK distributor: The Standard Manufacturing Co. – see entry.
Wessex Coppice Group Vale Farm, Smugglers Lane, Monkswood, Hampshire SO24 0HD Tel 01962 772030 Can put you in touch with companies and individuals working with coppiced hardwoods.
West Meters Phoenix House, London Road, Corwen, Denbighshire LL21 0DR Tel 01490 412004
Whichford Pottery See under Mail Order Companies, page 142.
Wilkinson Sword (Fiskars) Fiskars UK Ltd, Newlands Ave, Bridgend, Mid Glamorgan CF31 2XA, Wales Tel 01656 655595
Wolf Garden Ltd Crown Business Park, Tredegar, Gwent NP2 4ET, Wales Tel 01495 306600 www.wolf-garden.co.uk
Yeoman Solus Garden Leisure Group, Bromsgrove Road, Hunnington, Halesowen, West Midlands B62 0EW Tel 0121 504 2700 www.solusgl.com.
Zwilling JA Henckels UK distributor: Dexam International Ltd, Homebush Way, Midhurst West Sussex GU29 9HE Tel 01730 811888

retailers

There is a long tradition of the more specialist gardening tools and equipment being sold by mail-order retailers, and many of these companies now sell via the web. For basic items at reasonable prices, superstores such as Homebase and B&Q are worth considering but a good garden centre will offer the widest choice. Many home or department stores such as Heals, John Lewis, Habitat and the Conran Shop have outdoor living sections that are good for stylish containers and accessories.

MAIL-ORDER COMPANIES

Agralan Ltd The Old Brickyard, Ashton Keynes, Swindon, Wiltshire SN6 6QR Tel 01285 860015
agralan@cybermail.uk.com
Equipment for protection from weather and animals such as cloches, fleece and environmesh.
Agriframes Ltd Charlwoods Road, East Grinstead, West Sussex RH19 2HP Tel 01342 310000
www.agriframes.co.uk
Comprehensive catalogue of tools and sundries.
Andrew Crace Bourne Lane, Much Hadham, Hertfordshire SG10 6ER Tel 01279 842685
www.andrewcrace.com also www.alitags.com
Labels including alitags, topiary frames.
Arabella Lennox Boyd Garden Products Ltd
Gresgarth Hall, Caton, Lancaster LA2 9NB
Tel 01524 771838 www.arabellalennoxboyd.com
Small but select catalogue of well-designed items like cloches, wall fixings, some Sneeboer tools, asparagus knife, rain gauge.
CH Brannam Ltd Roundswell Industrial Estate, Barnstaple, Devon EX31 3NJ Tel 01271 343035
Pots sold via mail order; also has a factory shop.
Chandra Crafts Richardson's Farm, Crowhurst Lane, West Kingsdown, Kent TN15 6JE
Wooden tampers and cane tops.
Chelwood Tool Co. Thornbury, Bristol BS12 2JT
Tel 01454 413809
Manufacturers and suppliers of rakes.
Consumer Direct Ltd Lower St, Quainton, Aylesbury Buckinghamshire HP22 4BL Tel 01296 655217
Longrow cloches and cold frames.
Cranborne Stone West Orchard, Shaftesbury, Dorset SP7 0LJ Tel 01258 472685
Cast-stone containers.
Designs in Wood Foxwood Way, Chesterfield, Derbyshire S41 9RA Tel 01246 456120
www.designsinwood.co.uk
Wooden planters, troughs and windowboxes.
Diplex Ltd PO Box 172, Watford, Hertfordshire WD17 1BX Tel 01923 231784
Thermometers and rain gauges.
Dr Growgood Ltd PO Box 130, Terrington St Clement, King's Lynn, Norfolk PE34 4RH
Tel 01553 825710 www.drgrowgood.co
Sporks, container obelisks, plant supports.
Hallmark Identification Products 66 High St, Horsell, Woking, Surrey GU21 4SZ Tel 01483 772711
Plant labels.
Haxnicks Ltd Unit 8 Semley Industrial Estate, Station Road, Semley, Shaftsbury, Dorset SP7 9AN
Tel 01747 853939 www.haxnicks.co.uk
Solar bell cloches, root trainers.
Hortus Ornamenti 7 The Wren Centre, Westbourne Road, Emsworth, Hampshire PO10 7RN Tel 01243 374746 www.hortus-ornamenti.co.uk
Hand-crafted hand tools such as Jekyll weeder, forks and trowels.
J Toms Ltd Grigg Lane, Headcorn, Ashford, Kent TN27 9XT Tel 01622 891111.
Equipment for supporting and protecting trees.
LBS Group Standroyd mill, Cottontree, Colne, Lancashire BB8 7BW Tel 0870 7273616
Weather protectors, hand tools, pots, ties, storage.
Leakypipe Garden systems, White House Farm, Grundisburgh, Woodbridge, Suffolk IP13 6RR
Tel 01473 738280
Automatic watering systems.
Link-Stakes and Made to Last Upper Boddington, Daventry, Northamptonshire NN11 6DH
Tel 01327 260329 wwwlink-stakes.co.uk
Link-stakes and other plant supports.
Metal Art Works Priory Steps, Newtown, Bradford on Avon, Wiltshire, BA15 1NQ Tel 01225 865141
Contemporary metal trellis and edging.
Organic Gardening Catalogue Riverdene Business Park, Molesey Road, Hersham KT12 4RG
Tel 01932 253666 www.OrganicCatalog.com
Tools such as the ibis, and plant protection materials.
Plane & Simple Headcorn Road, Sutton Valence, Maidstone Kent ME17 3EH Tel 01622 842444
www.plane-and-simple.co.uk
Wooden obelisks and planters, wire products.
Rayment Unit 7, Hoo Farm, Monkton Road, Minster in Thanet, Kent CT12 4JB Tel 01843 821628
Ornate wire hanging baskets and planters.

Shore Hall Garden Designs Shore Hall, Cornish Hall End, Braintree, Essex CM7 4HW
Tel 01799 586225
Metal obelisks and plant supports.
Stuart Garden Architecture Burrow Hill Farm, Wiveliscombe, Somerset TA4 2RN
Tel 01984 667458 www.stuartgarden.com
Wooden trellis, obelisks and planters.
Suffolk Herbs Monks Farm, Coggeshall Road, Kelvedon, Essex CO5 9PG Tel 01376 572456
Seed company with a small selection of hand tools and cloches.
The Truggery Coopers Croft, Herstmonceux, East Sussex BN27 1QL Tel 01323 832314
www.truggery.fsnet.co.uk
Hand-made trugs.
Two Wests & Elliott Unit 4, Carrwood Road, Sheepbridge Industrial Estate, Chesterfield, Derbyshire S41 9RH Tel 01246 451077
www.twowests.co.uk
Strong on propagation tools and equipment.
WaterDance Creations Combe Cottage, Stortford Road, Leaden Roding, Near Dunmow, Essex CM6 1RB Tel 01279 876055 Info@waterdance-creations.co.uk
Ornamental sprinklers.
Whichford Pottery Whichford, Near Shipston-on Stour, Warwickshire CV36 5PG Tel 01608 684416
www.whichfordpottery.com
Hand-made traditional and contemporary terracotta pots.
Wiggly Wigglers Lower Blakemere Farm, Blakmere, Herefordshire HR2 9PX Tel 0800 216990
Can-o-worms and other composting systems.
Wolfin Textiles 64 Great Titchfield St, London W1W 7QH Tel 0207 636 4949
www.wolfintextiles.co.uk
Textile supplier that sells hessian by the metre.

WEBSITES
www.crocus.co.uk
Range of hand tools and interesting pots, including a selection from Eschbach.
www.dig-it.co.uk
Strong on contemporary containers. Also offers a mail-order service.
www.greenfingers.com
Wide range of tools and containers. Also offers a mail-order service.

GARDEN CENTRES AND GARDEN SHOPS
This is only a small selection of the many outlets available. To find a garden centre near you, try the Yellow Pages or www.martex.co.uk/hta, which has a directory of garden centres by county.

Wyevale Garden Centres Veldifer Lane, Kings Acre Road, Hereford, Herefordshire HR4 0SE
Tel 01432 276568 Store locator 0800 413213
www.wyevale.co.uk
The only national garden centre chain. Carries a range of garden tools, equipment and containers.

LONDON
Capital Gardens Ltd 1 Townsend Yard, Highgate Village, London N6 5JF Tel: 020 8348 5054
www.capitalgardens.co.uk
Part of a group of garden centres in North and South London and Berkhamsted.
The Chelsea Gardener 125 Sydney Street London SW3 6NR www.chelseagardener.com
Tel 0207 352 5656
Tools, containers and accessories.
Clifton Nurseries Ltd 5a Clifton Villas, Warwick Avenue, Maida Vale, London W9 2PH
Tel: 020 7289 6851 www.clifton.co.uk
Spear & Jackson tools plus range of terracotta pots.
Fulham Palace Garden Centre Bishops Avenue, Fulham, London SW6 6EE Tel: 020 7736 2640
www.angliangardener.co.uk
Good range of garden tools and equipment.
Jacqueline Edge 1 Courtnell Street, London W2 5BU
Tel 020 7229 1172
Ethnic pots, baskets, bamboo work.
Judy Green's Garden Store 11 Flask Walk, London NW3 1HJ Tel 020 7435 9757
Containers, small section of old hand tools, interesting plant labels.
Lloyd Christie Design & Manufacture
103 Lancaster Road, London W11 1QN
Tel 0207 243 6466 www.lloydchristie.com
Containers and obelisks.
RK Alliston 183 New Kings Road, Parsons Green, London SW6 4SW Tel: 020 7751 0077
www.rkalliston.com
Smart garden tools including Burgon and Ball items, and other garden accessories

SOUTH EAST
Aylett Nurseries North Orbital Road, London Colney, St Albans Herts AL2 1DH Tel 01727 822255
Wide range of gardening equipment and containers.
Fairalls 44 & 46 High St, Godstone, Surrey RH9 8LW
Tel 01883 742256 www.fairalls.co.uk
Landscaping equipment such as marker paint, pointing trowels, tape measures, builder's squares and spirit levels. Also protective clothing like goggles and ear defenders. Some garden tools.

Knights Nags Hall Nursery, Oxted Road, Godstone Surrey RH9 8DB Tel 01883 742275
www.knights-centres.co.uk
Full range of garden tools and equipment including brands such as Wolf, Bulldog, Gardena and Hozelock. Wide range of containers.
Snowhill Plant & Garden Centre Ltd
Snowhill Lane, Copthorne, West Sussex RH10 3EY
Tel 01342 712545 www.snowhill.co.uk
Opinel knives, trimmers, shredders and containers.
The Van Hage Garden Company Great Amwell, Ware, Hertfordshire SG12 9RP Tel: 01920 870811
www.vanhage.co.uk
Other branches at Bragbury End and Chenies.
Good range of garden tools and equipment.
Wolden Nurseries and Garden Centre
Cattlegate Road, Crews Hill, EN2 9DW
Tel: 020 8363 7003 www.woldens.co.uk
Wide selection of garden tools and equipment.

SOUTH WEST
Cadbury Garden Centre Smallway, Congresbury, Somerset BS19 5AA Tel 01934 876464
Good range of garden tools and equipment.
Endsleigh Garden Centre
Ivybridge, Devon PL21 9JL Tel 01752 898989
Wide range of garden tools and equipment.
Jacqueline Edge The Old Barn, Manor Farm, Chilmark, Wiltshire SP3 5AF Tel 01722 717800
Pots, baskets, bamboo work.

EAST ANGLIA
Bawdeswell Garden Centre East Dereham, Norfolk NR20 4RZ Tel 01362 688387
Good range of garden tools and equipment.
Notcutts Garden Centre
Ipswich Road, Woodbridge, Suffolk IP12 4AF
Tel: 01394 445400 www.notcutts.co.uk
Wide selection of garden tools and equipment including Wolf tools and their own Notcutts label.
Scotsdale Garden Centre
120 Cambridge Road, Great Shelford, Cambridge CB2 5JT Tel: 01223 842777
Good range of garden tools and equipment including Wilkinson Sword, Spear & Jackson and Wolf.

MIDLANDS
Queenswood Garden Centre Wellington, Hereford HR4 8BB Tel: 01432 830015 www.queenswood.co.uk
Felco secateurs, Burgon & Ball shears, Sandvik pruning tools, sporks and winged weeders.
Webbs of Wychbold Wychbold, Droitwich Spa, Worcestershire WR9 0DG Tel 01527 680000
Large selection of containers and equipment.
Jardinerie Kenilworth Road, Hampton in Arden, Solihull B92 0LP Tel 01675 442866
Garden tools and a range of contemporary pots.
Burford Garden Company Shilton Road, Burford, Oxford OX16 4PA Tel: 01993 823117
www.burfordgardencompany.co.uk www.bgc.co.uk
Good range of garden tools and equipment.

NORTHERN ENGLAND
Bridgemere Garden World Nantwich, Cheshire CW5 7QB Tel 01270 521100
Wide selection of garden tools and equipment.
Hayes Garden World Lake District Nurseries, Ambleside, Cumbria LA22 0DW Tel 015394 33434
Good range of garden tools and equipment.
Abbeydale Garden Company Abbeydale Road, South Dore, Sheffield South Yorkshire
Tel: 0114 236 9091 www.garden-glorious.com
Select range of garden tools including Burgon & Ball shears and winged weeders.

SCOTLAND
Dobbies Garden Centres plc Melville Nursery, Lasswade, Midlothian EH18 1AZ Tel 0131 663 1941
Good selection of garden tools and equipment.
Dobbies have 6 garden centres in Scotland.
Ben Reid & Co Ltd Countesswells Road, Aberdeen AB9 2QL Tel 01224 318744
Good selection of garden tools.
Klondyke Garden Centre Campus Roundabout, Kirkton Campus, Livingston EH54 7AW
Tel: 01506 410053 www.klondyke.co.uk
Wide selection of garden tools.

WALES
Jardinerie St Mellons Garden Centre, Newport Road, St Mellons, Cardiff, South Glamorgan CF3 9XH Tel: 02920 777977
Good range of garden tools and equipment.
Hurrans Garden Centre, Catsash Road, Langstone, Newport NP6 2LZ Tel: 01633 413355
Good selection of garden tools and equipment.

NORTHERN IRELAND
Ben Vista Nursery and Garden Centre
Ahogill, Ballymena, County Antrim BT42 2QT
Tel: 028 2587 1441
Wide range of garden tools and equipment.
Woodlawn Garden Centre Ltd 360 Saintfield Road, Belfast County Antrim BT8 4SJ Tel: 028 9040 1777
Good selection of garden tools and equipment.

index

A

Acer palmatum 'Sango-kaku' (Japanese maple), 61
add-on handles, 18
aerators, 135
    detachable hollow-tine, 125
    using, 126
African violets, 44
alliums, 39
    A. christophii, 38
    A. hollandicum 'Purple Sensation', 38, 39
Allen, Darina, 84
alpine trough, 97
anemones, 38
    A. blanda, 38
    A. nemorosa, 38
angle weeder, 23
anvil secateurs, 56
aquatic planters, flexible,104
Archer-Wills, Anthony, 28
asparagus knife, 70
Austin, David, 58

B

bag, large, 13
    mesh, 132
bark wrap, 88
basket, water-lily, 104
beech (Fagus sylvatica), 64
Begonia rex, 112
bell jars, 82–83
besom, 128
Bigfoot, the (for spade),13
billhook, 71
blanketweed, 28
blanket, electric 109
bonsai pot, 104
boots, 139
    walking, 139
    Wellington, 139
border fork, 14
border spade, 32
bow saw, 60–1
box (Buxus sempervirens), 67, 68
bromeliads, 68
broom, stiff, 128
bubble insulation, 86
buckets, 131
Buczacki, Stefan, 44
budding knife, 70
builder's square, 135
bulb planters, 34
    long-handled, 34
    quick-release, 34
    short-handled, 34
bulb planting, 37
    alliums, 38
    design, 38
    in rows, 37
    naturalizing in turf, 37
    starting in pots, 38

C

Calamagrostis x actuiflora 'Stricta', 101
cane caps, 77, 80
cane grip, plastic, 77
canes, bamboo, 78, 80
Canterbury fork, 19
capillary matting, 52
Carex buchananii, 102
caring for tools, 8
carrying sheet, 131
Carter, George, 68
cells, polystyrene, 107
cellular inserts, 106
chainlink strap, 79
Chatto, Beth, 24
chives, 72
Christies garden, Chelsea Flower Show, 68
Chusan palm (Trachycarpus fortunei), 101
circle hoe, 23
circular grove, 32
clay soil, working, 16
cleaning tools, 8
clear polythene, 82
Clematis, 76
    C. alpina, 76
    C. 'Edouard Desfosse', 76
    C. macropetala, 76
    C. 'Perle d' Azur', 76
clip, floral, 71
clipped, yew, 64
cloches, 82–3
    polycarbonate, 83
    round lantern, 83
    row, 83
    square lantern, 83
clogs, 139
cold frames, 82
comfort-fit secateurs, 56
compost bins, 53
    plastic, 53
    wooden (beehive), 53

compost, making, 54
compost scoop, 134
compost thermometer, 134
container obelisk, 74
containers, 89–104
core weeder, 27
corner planter, 97
curly hose and lance, 46
cut-and-come again salads and herbs, 72
cut-and-hold scissors, 71
cuttings, taking, 112
    hardwood, 112
    leaf, 112
cyclamen, 32
cylinder hand mower, 114

D

daffodils (Narcissus), 37, 72
dahlias, 101
deadheading flowers, 72
dephinums, 77, 80
dibbers, 34–5
    large wooden, 34
    l-shaped plastic, 34
    metal-tipped wooden, 34
    straight metal, 34
    using, 110
digging tools, 15
    duck-foot digger, 15
    heavy-duty hoe, 15
    mattock-pick, 15
    round-point shovel, 15
    square-point shovel, 15
digital thermometer, 134
domes, 88
dot-matrix shding, 86
draining spade, 13
draw hoe, basic, 23
drip irrigation, 48,
    setting up, 49
Druse, Ken, 94
duck-foot digger, 15
Dutch hoe, 23
    using, 24

E

ear defenders, 139
edger, half-moon, 117
edging shears, 117
    using, 118
elaeagnus, 101
elder (Sambucus nigra), 61
electric blanket, 109
electric hedgetrimmer, 63
electric lawn rake, 125
electric trimmer, 116
elephant (frame), 75
English Roses, 58
erigerons, 101

F

false topiary, 75
feeder, 50
fertilizer spreader, 126
    using, 126
fibreglass planter, 96
fibreglass pot, 93
fibreglass urn and pedestal, 93
fine mesh, 88
finial, terracotta, 77
firming the ground, 20
fist-grip trowel, 31
fleece, 86
    green, 86
    white, 86, 87
flexible netting, 78
floral clip, 71
flower basket, 131
flower pots, terracotta, 90
folding pruning saw, 60
forcing pots, 82–3
forcing rhubarb, 84
forks, 14
    border, 14
    Canterbury, 19
    hand, 26
    long-handled hand, 26
    manure or dung, 14
    potato, 14
    spork, 14
    stainless-steel garden, 14
    weeding, 26
frames, topiary, 75
fruit netting, 88

G

garden lines, 135
gauntlets, leather and suede, 138
gear secateurs, 56
gear-action loppers, 57
gear-action shears, 63
globe (topiary frame), 75
gloves, 138
    disposable, 138
    leather, 138
    nitrile-coated cotton, 138
    rubber, 138
    woolly, 138
goggles, 139

grabber hands, 128
grafting knife, 70
grass labyrinth, 122
grass parterre, 123
gravel garden, weeding, 24–5
greenhouse propagator, 109
growing from seed, 108
grow tubes, 107
guns, spray, 50
    adjustable, 50
    rose-head, 50

H

half tray, 106
hand mister, 43
hand rake, 18
hand-held spreader, 125
hanging baskets, 98
    basic wire, 98
    bracket, 98
    self-watering, 98
    wirework, 98
    wooden, 98
hardening off, 87
hardwood cuttings, 112
harvest knife, 70
hat, 139
hazel poles, 77
heavy clay soil, working, 16
hedgetrimmers, 63
    electric, 63
    rechargeable, 63
    using, 64
herb, or strawberry pot, 104
hessian, 86
hessian sacks, 132
Heuchera, 101
Hicks, Bobbi, 68
Hicks, Ivan, 68
Hobhouse, Penelope, 38
hoeing, 22
hoes, 22–23
    angle weeder, 23
    circle hoe, 23,
        using 24
    draw, 23
        basic, 23
        detachable, 23
    Dutch, 23
        using, 24
    heavy-duty, 15
    oscillating, 23
    onion, 23
        using, 24
    ridging, 23
    swoe, 23, 24
    three-pronged hand, 23
    two-pronged hand, detachable, 23
    Warren, 23
    winged weeder, 23
holster, 56
hose connectors, 47
    brass, 47
    double-check valve, 47
    4-way, 47
    plastic, 47
    repair, 47
hose reels, 47
    portable hose trolley, 47
    wall-mounted, 47
hoses, 46, 48
    curly hose and lance, 46
    seep, 48
    sprinkler, 48
household scissors, 71
hover mower, 115

I

ibis, 27, 28
ikebana shears, 71
indoor watering can, 42
interchangeable tool systems, 9
irrigation systems, 48–9
    gravity-fed, 48
Italian buckthorn (Rhamnus alaternus), 68

J

Japanese garden, raking sand and gravel in, 126

K

Keane, Marc Peter, 126
kneeler, 138
knee pads, 138
kneeling stool, 138
knife, weeding, 26
knives, 70–1
    asparagus, 70
    billhook, 71
    budding, 70
    grafting, 70
    harvest, 70
    ikebana shears, 71
    pruning, 70
    scalpel, 70

L

labels, punching, 40
lance, 50

landscaping rake, 18
lavender (Lavandula augustifolia), 67, 101
lawn design and maintenance, 121
lawn shears, 117
    multi shears, 117
leaf blower, powered, 128
leeks, planting, 40
levelling soil, 20
liners (for hanging baskets), 98
    moss, 98
    wool, 98
    plastic-backed wool, 98
link stakes, 78
long-handled hand fork, 26
long-handled trowel, 31
long tom, terracotta, 90
loop stakes, 78
loppers, 57
    bypass, 57
    gear-action, 57
    rachet, 57

M

materials for tools, 10
mattock-pick, 15
Maynard, Arne, 68
melianthus, 101
mowers, 114–5
    cylinder hand, 114
    hover, 115
    rechargeable, 115
    ride-on, 115
    rotary, 115
mowing a meadow, 118
multi shears, 117

N

net, pond, 27
netting
    flexible, 78
    fruit, 88
    pond, 88
    stiff, 78
    wire, 88
no-dig approach, 20
notched shears, 63
nozzles, spray, 50

O

obelisks, 74–6
    bamboo, 74
    container, 74
        using, 76
    metal, 74
        using, 76
    wooden, 74–5
        using, 76
Oudolf, Piet, 64, 68

P

paving weeder, 26
pea sticks, 77
peat pots, 106
pegs, 86
pelargoniums, 44
Pereire, Anita, 122
Phillyrea latifolia, 68
    P. angustifolia, 68
phormium, 87
plant labels, 35
    aluminium, 35
    copper, 35
    punching kit for, 35
    plant rings, 79
plant supports, simple, 77
    hazel poles, 77
    pea sticks, 77
    tree stake, 77
plant ties, 79
    chainlink strap, 79
    natural string, 79
    plant ring, 79
    plastic ties, 79
    polypropylene twine 79
    raffia, 79
    rose tie, 79
    supersoft tree tie, 79
    tree tie with buckle, 79
    velcro, 79
planters
    corner, 97
    fibreglass, 96
    herb, 104
    metal, 97
    Versailles, 96
planting a large pot, 94
planting and staking a tree, 80
planting in small spaces, 32
planting tools, 34–5
pointed shovel, 16
pointing trowel, 27
pole pruner, 57
Pollan, Michael, 118
polythene, 86
    black, 86
    clear, 86
    knitted, 86
ponds, weeding, 28
potato fork, 14

pots, large, 92–4
  angle-top, 93
  cast-stone, 93
  fibreglass, 93
  glazed ceramic, 92
  metal, 91
  planting, 94
  plastic, 90
  plastic tub, 92
  terracotta, 90, 92
  terrazzo, 91
  wall, 91
  see also propagating pots and
    trays
preparing a seedbed, 20
pressure sprayer, 43
  knapsack, 43
  with lance, 43
pricking out, 108
propagating pots and trays, 106
  cellular inserts, 106
  grow tubes, 106
  half tray, 106
  peat pots, 106
  polystyrene cells, 106
  quarter tray, 106
  root trainers, 106
  round pot, 106
  seed tray, 106
  square pot, 106
  terracotta seed pan, 106
propagators, 109
  electric blanket, 109
  greenhouse, 109
  windowsill, 109
protection from cold winds, 87
pruning, 58
  English roses, 58
  mature trees, 58
  twiggy shrubs, 58
pruning knife, 70
pruning saw, 60
  folding, 60
  using, 61
punching labels, 40

Q
quarter tray, 106

R
raffia, 79
rain diverter, 52
rain gauge, 134
rain water, 52
rakes (cultivating), 18–20
  basic garden, 18
    using, 20
  bow, detachable, 18
  flower, detachable, 18
  hand, 18
  landscaping, 18
  using, 20
rakes (lawns and other surfaces),
    124–5
  bamboo, 124
  electric lawn, 125
  hay, 125
  plastic, detachable, 124
  rubber, 124
  sand, 124
  scarifier, detachable, 124
  self-cleaning, 124
  small, detachable, 124
  spring-tine, 124
    using, 126
raking sand and gravel in a Japanese
    garden, 126
recycling, 53
reels (hose), wall-mounted, 47
repairing tools, 8
rhubarb, forcing, 84
ring stake, 78
rootcutter, 60, 61
root trainers, 107
rose tie, 79
Roses, English, 58
  'Sophy's Rose', 58
rosemary (Rosmarinus officinalis), 67

S
sand rake, 124
saws, 60–1
  bow saw, 60
  folding pruning saw, 60
  root cutter, 60
  saw attachment, 60
  scabbard, 60
    using, 61
scabbard 60
scalpel, 70
scissors, 70–1
  cut and hold, 71
  household, 71
scythe, 117
  using, 118
secateurs, 56–7
  anvil, 56
  bypass, 56
  comfort-fit, 56
  gear, 56

holster for, 56
rachet, 56
seed bed, preparing, 20
seed drill, making, 20
seed pan, terracotta, 106
seed sower, 110
seed tray, 106
seep hoses, 44, 48
Senecio cineraria 'White Diamond', 101
servicing tools, 8
sharpening tools, 8
shears (pruning), 62–3, 71
  gear-action, 63
  hedge, 64
  ikebana, 71
  notched, 63
  swivel, 63
  telescopic, 63
  trimming, 63
shears (lawn), 116–8
  edging, 117
    using, 118
  multi, 117
sheet materials, 86
  black polythene, 86
  bubble insulation, 86
  clear polythene, 86
  dot-matrix shading, 86
  green fleece, 86
  hessian, 86
  knitted polyethylene, 86
  pegs, 86
  sheet mulch, 86
  white fleece, 86
shovels, 15
  round-point, 15
  square-point, 15
shredder, 53
shrub shelter, 88
shrubs, 58
  pruning, 58
  renovating, 58
sickle, 117
  using, 118
sieves
  for making compost, 53
  for propagating, 110
silver birch (Betula pendula), 72
single digging, 16
snake's-head fritillary (Fritillaria
    melagris), 37
soil-testing kit, 135
  using 136
sowing seed, 108
space-saving tools, 9
spades (digging), 12–13
  draining, 13
  modern long-handled, 13
  stainless-steel, 13
  traditional, 13
  traditional long-handled 13
spades (planting), 30–1
  modern border, 20
  traditional border, 30
spiral, metal (plant support), 77
  using, 76
spiral (topiary frame), 75
spirit level, 135
spork, 14
spot weeder, 27
spray nozzle, 50
sprayers, 43
  hand mister, 43
  knapsack, 43
  pressure with lance, 43
  pressure, 43
spreaders, 125
  hand-held, 125
  wheeled rotary, 125
spring-tine rake, 124
sprinkler hoses, 44, 48
sprinklers, 50–1
  mobile, 51
  ornamental, 51
  oscillating, 50
  pulse-jet, 50
  rotating, 50
  static, 50
stakes, 78
  link, 78
  loop, 78
  ring, 78
stem guard, 88
storing tools, 9, 132
strawberry, or herb pot, 104
string, natural, 79
supersoft tree tie, 79
supporting perennials, 80
sweet peas (Lathyrus odoratus), 76
swoe, 23, 24

T
taking cuttings, 112
tampers, 111
tape measure, 135
taproot weeder, 26
tension bolts, 78
terracotta finial, 77
terracotta containers, 90–1
  flower pots, 90

large pot, 92
long tom, 90
seed pan, 106
window box, 99
testing the soil, 136
thermometers, 134
  compost, 134
  digital, 134
  maximum–minimum, 134
  soil, 134
  using, 134
three-pronged cultivator, 19
three-pronged hand hoe, 23
tiller, detachable four-star, 19
tomatoes, 44, 45
tool belt, 139
tool construction methods, 10
tools for a productive garden, 84
topiary, 62, 67–8
topiary frames, 75
  elephant, 75
  globe and spiral, 75
topiary shears, 63
training young trees, 72
tree stake, 77
tree tie with buckle, 79
trellis, 74–5
  metal, 75
  wooden trellis, 75
trimmers, 116
  electric, 116
  rechargeable, 116
troughs, 96
  alpine, 97
  plastic, 97
  wooden, 97
trowels, 30–1
  fist-grip, 31
  long-handled, 31
  narrow-width, 31
  pointing, 27
  right-angled, 31
  standard-width, 31
trug, light, 131
tulips (Tulipa), 37, 38
  planting, 40
twine, polypropylene, 79

U
Uncina rubra, 101
urns, 92–3
  cast-stone, 93
  fibreglass, and pedestal, 93

V
velcro (plant ties), 79
Versailles planter, 96

W
walking boots, 139
wall fixings, 78
wall pots, 91
  glazed, 91
  plastic, 91
  wicker, 91
water butt, wall-mounted, 52
Warren hoe, 23
water barrel, round, 52
watering, 44
  container-grown plants, 94
  young plants, 44
  quick, 44
  seedlings, 44
watering cans, 42–3
  brass rose, 42
  indoor, 42
  metal long-reach, 42
  plastic long-reach, 42
  traditional metal, 42
  using, 40
watering systems, 49
water-lily basket, 104
water storage, 52
water timers, 47
  advanced, 47
  simple, 47
weeders, 26–7
  core, 27
  paving, 26
  pond , 27
  spot, 27
  taproot, 26
  winged, 23
weeding
  and planting, 28
  between paving, 28
  between plants, 28
  gravel garden, 24
  lawn, 28
  paving, 26
  ponds, 28
weeping willow, 58
wellington boots, 139
wheelbarrow, 130
widgers, 110
  plastic, 110
  steel, 110
Williams, Paul, 101
windowboxes, 99
  aluminium, 99
  balcony bracket, 99
  plastic, 99
  terracotta, 99
  wooden, 99
winter pansies, 101
wire, galvanized, 78
wormery, 53
  setting up, 54

Y
yew (Taxus)
  clipped, 64
  topiary, 67, 68

author's acknowledgements

I would especially like to thank Stuart Cooper, who approached me to write this book, and who at all times has been supportive, thorough and patient. Thanks also to Jacqui Small, who put together such an experienced team to help steer me through the project. Robin Rout deserves special mention for the flair and efficiency of his art direction and design. I am grateful to Craig Knowles for the care he took both with the studio photography and for his inspirational shots of the gardening techniques. Many thanks to all the companies who lent items for photography and to John Crummay and his staff for helping to unpack, store and return them. In particular, I would like to thank Brian Knight of Knights Garden Centre, Nags Hall Nursery, who lent many of the containers photographed. I am indebted to my friend Ruth Chivers who provided me with contacts, sources and information, and also much moral support. My appreciation and thanks go to the garden writers and designers featured in the book who were so generous with their time: Darina Allen, Anthony Archer-Wills, David Austin, Stefan Buczacki, George Carter, Beth Chatto, Ken Druse, Ivan Hicks, Penelope Hobhouse, Marc Peter Keane (www.mpkeane.com), Mary Moody, Piet Oudolf, Anita Pereire, Michael Pollan, Nori and Sandra Pope, and Paul Williams. Also, thanks to the picture researcher Emily Hedges who located the garden photographs so efficiently. Finally, a big thank you to my husband Stephen and my daughters Caroline, Helena and Nicole for putting up with me not being there as much as I should have been.

publisher's acknowledgements

We would like to thank the following for supplying photographs for this book::

p9 Hugh Palmer/Oare House, p17 Steven Wooster/Hadspen Garden, p21 Hugh Palmer/Hambleton Hall, p25 Jerry Harpur/des: Beth Chatto, p29 Andrew Lawson/Stile House/designer: Anthony Archer-Wills, p39 Jerry Harpur/Park Farm Essex, designer: Jill Cowley, p45 Jerry Harpur, p59 David Austin Roses (Sophy's Rose), p65 Jerry Harpur/designer: Piet Oudolf, p68 top Steven Wooster/Evolution/Gardens Illustrated, RHS Chelsea Flower Show 2000/designers: Piet Oudolf and Arne Maynard, bottom Jerry Harpur/designer: Bobbi Hicks, NSW, Australia, p69 Marianne Majerus/The Christies Sculpture Garden, RHS Chelsea '99/designer: George Carter, p76 left Andrew Lawson, top right Clive Nichols, bottom right Clive Nichols/Ralph Cade/Robin Green, p85 Stephen Robson/Ballymaloe Cookery School, Co. Cork, Ireland, p95 Jerry Harpur/designer: Richard Hartlage, p101 left Jerry Harpur/Oliver Roof Garden/designer: Edwina Von Gal, centre right Clive Nichols/designer: Stephen Woodhams, bottom right Nicola Browne/designer: Jinny Blom, p119 John Peden/designer: Michael Pollan, p122, 123 Andrew Lawson/designer: Anita Pereire, p127 Jerry Harpur/designer: Marc Peter Keane.

tools for gardeners